My Happy Feet

Memoirs of a Twenty-Seven Year
Journey With Parkinson's Disease

Ruth Anne Drown

Scripture taken from the NEW AMERICAN STANDARD BIBLE®, Copyright © 1960,1962,1963,1968,1971,1972,1973,1975,1977,19 95 by The Lockman Foundation. Used by permission

Lulu Publishing Services rev. date: 05/29/2018

"Mom, you should write a book and call it,
'My Happy Feet'"

CONTENTS

$\mathcal{F}$oreword

I am not a famous movie star, comedian, or gold medal winning athlete. I have done nothing that would bring me fame or fortune. But, I believe that I have something to share with a specific group of people; a group of people who have all been initiated into a select club, so to speak, whose members never asked or wanted to join. It is actually a club that we would like to escape from. A club that we wish we had never heard of. The name of this club is called "Parkinson's Disease." I will refer to this select group of people as PLWP (people living with Parkinson's). I write my story for all the millions of brave people around the world fighting this disease with their loved ones, friends, researchers, and physicians. I write for all those who have been inducted into this "club" and are trying to manage this disease.

As I share my story, I include many details of early symptoms, diagnosis, treatment, personal strategies, and emotions, of trying to manage this eventually crippling disease. My journey has been a twenty-six year progression, since my diagnosis in 1990. I was thirty-seven years old. I write hoping that it will help someone else who is also just a regular person like me, whose life, and the lives of their families have been permanently altered by this mean, deteriorating, brain disease.

I dedicate this book to my family and friends…My Mom and Dad, my husband, Jeff, my three children, Stephen, Elizabeth, and Megan, my daughter in law Jessica, son-in law Christopher, our amazing grandsons, Nicholas, John, Thomas, and our beautiful granddaughter Jillian. Thank you for your love, support, patience, and encouragement. Thank you for still seeing me for who I really am, not just as the disease.

A special thank you to my youngest daughter, Megan whose idea it was that I write my story and call it "My Happy Feet."

$\mathcal{M}$y Happy Feet

My story has a very unremarkable, but happy beginning for me. I will start at the point of my last memories of normalcy, and a life that was unfettered by the vision of what was to come. I was a young wife and mother....well, maybe not that young, but compared to where I am at now, thirty- seven is pretty young. I was Jeffrey's wife, and mom to three beautiful children. My son, Stephen, was ten years old. My daughter, Elizabeth was eight years old, and my baby Megan was only twenty months old. We were basically a loving, happy, healthy, church going family, living and growing up in suburban New Jersey.

We were very active in our non-denominational Christian church, teaching Sunday school, singing in the choir, going to Bible studies, and fellowshipping with our dear friends. I also played the piano for the church choir, as well as taught private piano lessons at home.

As our lives progressed, we were kept busy with our children's education, sports, music, etc. The days were filled with laughter, and typical family activities. I guess you could say that even with our ups and downs, life was good before the winter of 1989, when an unexplainable darkness starting seeping into my life.

It started out very insidiously, and yet suddenly at the same time. Although these two words sound like an oxymoron, that is how it felt to me. Several years went by as I tried to deal with the subtle changes that were taking place in me, physically and emotionally.

In the very early stages it felt like a depression. I had terrible intrusive thoughts that I could not seem to control. My baby was twenty months old, and I had just stopped nursing her. I felt as if I was going crazy. My husband and parents were extremely concerned. I started feeling very anxious. When I played the piano, I would shake all over. I thought I was having stage fright for no reason. I started to look differently; my face had no expression. When I walked, people would comment that I didn't swing my right arm, and it looked as if I was dragging my right foot. I had no clue that I was exhibiting all of these signs, or symptoms. My right arm didn't seem to work right. I had difficulty washing my hair, brushing my teeth, playing the piano, and giving Megan a bath. But, I continued trooping on, pretending that it was nothing. I was just going through something, and it would go away as quickly as it came.

Well, it didn't. The negative thoughts kept attacking my mind, and my motor skills were getting worse and worse. My brother commented to me one day, "Ruth, what happened to the bounce you used to have in your step?" I didn't know; it just went away. I was so sad. I started using my left hand more and more. A friend commented one Sunday as I was wiping off a table after a church dinner, "Ruth, I thought you were right handed." I even wondered, "Why wasn't I using my right hand?" I just knew it didn't work properly.

I decided that I should make an appointment with a psychologist, because I was going crazy. So, I made an appointment with a psychologist. She was a very nice woman and probably meant well. She told me that I was having postpartum depression. She explained the reason I had this was because I stopped nursing my baby and that those "good feeling, motherly" hormones were going away. "Oh great," I thought. "You mean I'm not going to love my kids anymore?" No way! Then she wanted to take me back to my childhood and figure out why I was depressed. I was not in the mood to go back to my childhood. She wanted to start me on meds. I declined the offer, and couldn't wait to get out of there. I knew these suggestions, were not what was bothering me. I did, however, still think I was "cracking up," or having some sort of nervous breakdown.

My next step was inspired by my mother, suggesting that maybe it was something physical that was causing these dark feelings, anxiety, and the newest symptom of feeling like I was shaking all the time, and yet felt paralyzed…..very hard to explain.

I went to my general doctor for a check-up. I was literally shaking all over. He gave me a thorough physical examination, including EEG, EKG, chest X-ray, blood tests, Pap smear, and you name it. After we were finished and all the tests were checked off negatively, he sat me down in a chair in his office and said, "Well, Mrs. Drown I can't really find anything wrong. As far as the tests go, you're pretty healthy."

However, he then made me do something strange. He told me to walk across his office and then he had me write my name on a piece of paper. He asked me if my handwriting looked normal. I mentioned that for some reason it looked really small. I usually have large flowing handwriting. The next thing he said was, "I want you to see a neurologist. I think I see something here." He did not say what it was that he saw, but I knew he knew what he saw. He also said that I wasn't going crazy. That is all I needed to hear. I immediately made an appointment with a neurologist.

I'm pretty sure I went by myself. The only thing I can remember is feeling very shaky and nervous. I was still under the impression that I was a nervous wreck. The neurologist had me do all kinds of weird things, like touching each of my fingers to my thumb, tapping my feet on the floor, walking around the little room, and trying to touch my forefingers together the way a police officer would have a person who has been pulled over for a DUI. He also checked my reflexes, and moved my arm up and down from the elbow, so that it would be at a 90 degree angle and then straight out in front of me. What the Dr. was looking for was something called "staccato" movement as he gently pulled my arms and hands up and down. As a musician, I know exactly what this term means in music. It is a note that is struck or plucked in a very quick movement. In a person with PD It feels like a quick jerking movement, as if the arm was trying to pull back from the doctor pulling it. Just like the hand pulls back and plucks the keys of a stringed instrument using a staccato technique.

It was not a super long appointment, but it didn't take him long to make a diagnosis. He said, "Based on my clinical observation, I see a little Parkinson's." At the time, I didn't know what he meant by, a "little" Parkinson's. I think I do now, which will come a little later in my story.

I was confused because I thought PD was an "old people's" disease. After all, I was the mother of three children, one of whom was under the age of two years old. What was he talking about? I was more mortified than afraid. This brought to mind an embarrassing vision which you could only imagine. I had seen a documentary on one of those TV programs like 60 Minutes or Dateline NBC which showed a video with a woman, who had Parkinson's, in the midst of terrible dyskinesia which are the involuntary movement of muscles due to side effects of medication. It consists of a writhing body. It usually begins in the feet, then legs, and can eventually involve the whole body. A person will twist and squirm, and the person usually puts effort into fighting the movements, which is extremely difficult and sometimes painful. I had thought to myself that this was the most horrible thing, and man I'm glad I didn't have that. I couldn't have known that this scene was my future being played out for me.

My doctor mentioned that society is seeing more and more young people who are developing Parkinson's disease. At this point in the examination, I asked a lot of questions, none of which he could give me any concrete answers to, which he was very unapologetic for. The two big questions I had were as follows: "What caused it?" and, "What is my prognosis?" His response was in order.

"We don't know," and "We can't tell you how Parkinson's disease, will manifest itself in your future. You may live with mild symptoms for twenty years, or you could be in a wheelchair in five years. We just don't know. Parkinson's disease is specially designed for each person who has it."

How nice, a specially designed disease just for me. Each patient may have one, two, or three symptoms in common with another patient with PD, but no two Parkinson's patients look exactly the same. Although there are many varying symptoms, and changes with the progression of the disease, the symptoms that most people have in early Parkinson's include tremor, stiffness, rigidity, and problems with gait of walking, such as walking slowly and deliberately, shuffling feet, and eventually the freezing of gait. Other symptoms are less obvious such as depression, anxiety, and sleeplessness.

My first main symptom was rigidity. Following that, my gait became affected. My family and friends noticed this before I did. I was jogging with my husband, and he asked me why I didn't swing my right arm when I walked or ran. I didn't know what he was talking about. Then others noticed that I was kind of dragging my right leg. I still didn't have a clue. Next, my limbs just did not work properly. My legs felt as If they weighed 100 lbs. each. As mentioned before, there was that friend who commented why I was using my left hand instead of my right hand to wipe a table. That was really strange, but very observant of him. As time went by, my right side was definitely affected first. It is still the weaker side.

Things were becoming very difficult. I developed serious trembling in my legs; it was getting difficult to brush my teeth and wash my hair. One thing I did not have, nor do I have as of this writing, is the terrible and sometimes violent "at rest" tremors that many PD patients have. I am very grateful for that. However, still writing about my early symptoms, I truly knew that something was seriously wrong with me.

I digress back to my first neurology exam. In answer to my first question, "What caused this?" The answer was, "That is the million dollar question. If we knew what caused it, we could probably cure it." He suggested a few causes like pesticides or genetics. My mind started racing back to when the kids were little; we used to go camping. Every night, it seemed, after we had just gotten our campfire cooked dinner on the picnic table, the mosquito spraying vehicle came around causing a huge pesticide cloud to cover the area. Another vision that came to me was that I used to have a big vegetable garden and I would use a supposedly "organic" insecticide on my vegetables. Perhaps I didn't clean the vegetables good enough and I was unknowingly poisoning myself. Perhaps I have a genetic factor and a predisposition to PD, and I inherited it from some old ancestor who shook, and nobody knew why back in those days.

I already addressed the neurologist's answer to my second question about my prognosis. He just didn't know. It could go very well for a long time, or very badly in a short time. He was very nice and extremely intelligent. I'm surprised I could understand any of what he said. I really didn't understand much of what he was saying neurologically at all. It is a complicated, degenerative, brain disease. How could I understand? I just know how I felt. So, he sent me out of his office with a prescription for a drug called "Sinemet" and a prescription for an MRI, just to make sure I didn't have a brain tumor, or signs of a stroke. At the time, I embarrassingly admit that I would have preferred one of those two diseases. God forgive me, but they sounded better than this old person shaky disease called Parkinson's. This diagnosis was like receiving a life sentence. There is no known cure. The neurologist said, "It won't kill you, but it will make your life miserable." Talk about brutal honesty. There are, however, complications of Parkinson's, whether acerbated by medication, or other health issues, that a person can succumb to.

I was the epitome of dazed and confused. It was almost as if I didn't feel anything. I didn't even cry. I wasn't angry. I dare say I wasn't even feeling.... emotionally that is.

After that first appointment, I went directly to my parents' house, where my entire family was gathered including all the children. I didn't include the children in the conversation to follow because I didn't think that they had really picked up on my subtle changes yet, at least not to my knowledge. They never said anything, but I know that children pick up on more than we think they do. We have three very astute children. At this time, their ages were about two and a half, eight, and ten. Believe it or not, my parents were relieved that it was a suspected case of PD and not something worse. However, my husband and I were in complete denial. After all, I was too young!!

In the days and weeks following, I had many conflicting emotions. The most disturbing thought that kept coming back to me was, "What if the neurologist was right and I did end up in a wheelchair in five years or so." That was not acceptable to me. It scared me and made me vow to fight this prediction with all that was in me. I started taking the Sinemet just to prove that I didn't have P D. However, it began working about twenty minutes after my first pill. It was glorious. I felt relatively normal. It was beyond imagination. I hadn't felt like this is so long. I was back to myself. I wasn't shaking. I didn't feel nervous, or depressed. My negative thoughts were gone. Just like that! The Sinemet worked like a charm. "This is great," I thought. "Even though I don't have Parkinson's, for some reason this medicine is working for me."

So, I took my Sinemet faithfully. I was doing everything I could do before I developed my first symptom relating to side effects of the Sinemet. This happened about two years later.

When I went back to the neurologist for one of my follow-up appointments, he could see that I was in deep denial and recommended that I see a "Movement Disorders" specialist. "Oh great," I thought. "I feel fine. Why stir something up? After all, the Sinemet was working great." That is exactly why. He told me that the medicine only works because I have Parkinson's. It was covering up all my symptoms.

He made an appointment for me to see a brilliant Movement Disorders specialist at Robert Wood Johnson University Hospital. Unfortunately, I had to go off the medicine so that the new doctor could see me in my "other state." Not much time went by at all before I was transformed into the shaky, scared, nervous, paralyzed person, with the vacant expression on my face. The specialist didn't take very long to come up with the same diagnosis. He spent a very long time examining me, which I liked. Many questions were asked and answered as best as he could. More Cat scans and MRIs were taken. He added another drug in addition to the Sinemet. This drug was supposed to slow down the progression of the loss of dopamine in the brain.

At this point in my story, I think it would be a good time to explain exactly what I understand about the scientific biological aspects of Parkinson's disease. I will really try to keep it simple. I am not a scientist, but I am an intelligent person, and I needed to understand what was happening to me. Maybe then I could explain it to other people. So here goes my attempt to explain in my own words something that is so complicated and yet simple, another oxymoron. It deals with such infinitesimal pieces of energy, chemicals, and cells firing back and forth, and the effect they have on the brain's connection to nerves and muscles. There is this chemical called dopamine (a neurotransmitter) which is produced by brain nerve cells that are located in a tiny part of the brain called the substantia nigra pars, located in the basal ganglia. This tiny part of the brain is responsible for movement and so much more. For some reason these cells begin dying in people with PD, and the dopamine gradually diminishes. Dopamine is the "all powerful" messenger that allows the nerves and muscles to move properly. I have read that before a person is even diagnosed with PD, they have lost somewhere around 80% of dopamine in their brain. I know this is extremely simplified, but it's the best I can do. I know there's a lot more to it, but all I need to know is that my brain has dopamine, which makes my body move, gives me the ability to walk, talk, eat, think, and function, and my dopamine is running low, really low. I need to replace it, and keep it from running out altogether. Thus enters the drug Sinemet, whose generic name is Carbidopa /Levodopa. That has been the Holy Grail of Parkinson's treatment for the last forty to fifty years; more about this later.

Oddly enough, the only way a doctor can announce a diagnosis of Parkinson's is simply by clinical observation. There is no blood test that would indicate it. There are no other tests that can indicate it. The only thing that will reveal concrete evidence of Parkinson's disease is an autopsy. The area of the basal ganglia will look different. After that autopsy, it cannot be denied anymore. The person actually **had** Parkinson's.

My new doctor wanted all new Cat scans and MRIs. So I had to go through that all over again. I never knew I was claustrophobic, but anyone would feel claustrophobic in that MRI tube. It wasn't necessarily the smallness of the space, but rather the sound inside of it. It sounded like a jackhammer was pounding my brain. I got through it by listening to Beethoven's "Adagio in C minor" through head phones, and in my mind trying to quote every Bible verse that I had ever memorized. I constantly repeated the words from Psalms 139.

"O Lord, where can I go from your spirit? Where can I hide from your face? If I say surely the darkness will overwhelm me......and the light around me will become night.....even the darkness is not dark to you and the night is as bright as the day. Darkness and light are alike to you.....for you formed my inward parts, and weaved me together in my mother's womb. I will give thanks to you for I am fearfully and wonderfully made. Wonderful are your works, and my soul knows it very well."

I think remembering this Psalm, and the fact that God was with me and knew what He was doing when he created me in my mother's womb, was the beginning of my acceptance. However, I still had a long way to go. The next step was to get a Cat-scan. I'm not sure why, but it must show different things. When I went for the Cat-scan, they gave me iodine dye in my veins. This procedure makes it easier to see the brain images clearly. The only problem was that I didn't know that I am allergic to iodine dye. I know now! As the liquid dye was being sent through my veins, I started getting hot all over, and my lips began to feel like the size of Texas. Then I started itching all over my body. The technician must have been looking somewhere else because she didn't notice until I said, "Um, excuse me I think there's something wrong with my lips."

Woops, Now I was having a severe allergic reaction. The next step could have been anaphylactic shock. Oh boy, this was just what I needed. So, they quickly got me out of the Cat-scan and made me drink gallons of water to flush the dye out of my system. This nearly exploded my bladder. After some time, we left the imaging place, stopped at a gas station so I could relieve myself and then picked up our kids from school. We acted as if nothing had happened at all. We were still good at hiding the truth of the matter, or so we continued to think.

When all the new test results came back negative, as we all knew that they would, I began to realize that after all, I probably did have Parkinson's disease; however, complete acceptance was still several years away. At this point, I began to think about my future. The thoughts that made me finally cry out in desperation were, "Will I be able to stand up at my children's high school and college graduations?" Between our first child and third child there are nine years. That is way past the five year wheelchair possibility. "Will I be able to dance and sing at our children's weddings? Will I be able to hold, love, and take care of my first grandchild or grandchildren, if God blesses our family in such a wonderful way? Will I be a burden to my husband and children? Will I be able to take care of my parents as they grow older? What will I look like? What will I do? Will I have to give up piano teaching? Will everyone still love me? Will I sound strange, look strange, and weird?" There were so many questions which were only the tip of the iceberg. "Really, what does my future hold?" Most of these questions will have been answered as of this writing.

The future, which is now the not so distant past, had always seemed so bright and clear; now seemed unsure and alien to me. All the things I had been looking forward to doing with my family seemed shrouded in mystery and fog. This caused such an unbearable sadness and despair deep within my soul; a feeling which I had never known before.

As I type this many years later, it still brings tears to my eyes and a nauseous feeling in the pit of my stomach. I never balled up my fist and raised it in anger to God I never even asked "Why me?" I know better than that. I honestly said to myself, "Why not me?" I'm not immune to heartbreak, even though I have had a pretty wonderful life. Who am I that I should be free from pain? I am just one of God's children who is going through something, just like millions and millions of others. We all have our pain to bear and things to deal with. I just have to figure out how I am going to manage this insidious disease. As someone who studies the Bible, I know that God allows certain things to come into our lives for reasons that we simply do not understand now. I knew this in the early days of PD in my head, but in my heart I was still heartbroken that my Heavenly Father would even allow this to happen. The hurt came from the fact that I would protect my children from any pain or suffering that I could humanly protect them from. I would die for them. Surely my heavenly father would desire to protect me from all pain and tribulation. Even my parents were deeply distressed over my condition. They would have cut off a limb if they knew it would heal me.

In hindsight, I realize after many years that God does love me enough to die for me, as I would for my children. All of my suffering, as well as all of humanity's suffering was crucified with Christ on the cross. I don't need to fear my future because there is joy to come when earthly sorrow, pain, suffering, and even earthly love and joy will be over and I will spend eternity with Him. I truly believe this, and am looking forward to my new body. He promised me this in His Word.

You may wonder if I ever thought that God could heal me if He wanted to. I believe that He could heal me. After over twenty-five years of living with PD, I believe that a greater testimony of my faith is to be an inspiration to others, while living with Parkinson's. Would I like to be healed? No brainer. Of course I would. I have been on my knees with my head to the floor begging for healing. I have poured out my heart to God. I have had pastors and others lay hands on me, fervently praying with all love and sincerity for God to heal me. It has never been totally realized in my life. I say totally, because in a way I feel healed in my spirit. I am confident that I can be of greater use to God and other people with Parkinson's disease. It gives me a passion to help others, and those afflicted with other physical as well as mental ailments can relate to me and identify with me.

Family Life and Parkinson's

I was in the process of editing my story, but as I read it, I had become aware of the fact that I really didn't go into much detail regarding much about the life of our young family: what it was like as a young mother and my husband, a young father, dealing with a degenerative disease, like Parkinson's. I share this part of my life, our lives, because it's about my family. How did I pull off being my best self, a mother and wife when every day I was assaulted by a monster? I share because there is hope. There is still a way to live, love, laugh, and take care of your family after a terrible diagnosis of not only Parkinson's but other debilitating diseases that people struggle with on a daily basis. A few of these diseases come to mind, like Multiple Sclerosis, Fibromyalgia, Crones, Lupus, Lyme's to mention a few. I know there are so many more. It wasn't easy, but it's all I had.

My main strategy was get up, take my meds, wait for them to kick in, put on my make-up, dedicate through prayer, my day to God, eat breakfast, wake up the kids, get them off to school, and try to just keep functioning. In the process, I pretended that I was normal, and I just moved on and remained the positive person I have always been. It was, almost as if it didn't exist. I know that sounds really strange, and this was way after I wasn't in denial anymore. I just felt that presenting an appearance of normalcy was important for our children. This attitude sort of back fired on me, as you will read later on. But for the most part, it seemed to work while the kids were growing up. No matter how bad I felt, I just plowed through and kept smiling.

When our children were in school, we were very busy with their education, friends, our family, and church. I never missed a "Back to School Night," a flute, guitar, gymnastics, ballet lesson, band concerts, Christmas concerts, art shows, football games, wrestling matches, band competition, class trips to museums, farms, Ellis Island and the Statue of Liberty. I was class mother when each child was in kindergarten. We rarely ever missed Sunday school or church on Sundays, even after a busy week. We tried to put the example of putting God first in our lives, and the life of our family.

I would however, sometimes dread these events, because you never knew how or when my "extracurricular" body movements would occur. They were much milder back then so I could disguise them more. I would tell most people at this point about my affliction, only if they asked. Most of our friends and acquaintances became genuinely upset when I told them. As usual, I would say that I was fine and coping with it, which I guess I really was. So I hated when they felt sorry for me. I am so sensitive to people who tend to pity me. I just want to be treated the way any person wants to be treated. I felt like a freak as it was, so I wanted to be treated as if I wasn't a freak. I know this sounds ridiculous, but it was part of my processing my identity as a Parkinsonian.

Needless to say, that even with this monkey on my back, our family enjoyed our times being together despite PD. We did what everyone does. We took a family vacation to Disneyworld, shortly after my diagnosis. We had a great time, and PD's appearance was still fairly benign.

We spent a week on Lake Winnipesaukee, in New Hampshire, where it rained the entire week. We never even went into the water. The cottage was filthy. Jeff and I had two cots with wheels on the bottom as our beds. Great nights.... The girls screaming because of spider webs and bugs in their room. Jeff and I were rolling around on our cots trying to sleep, and Stephen was complaining that we needed to rent a boat for the week; not the best vacation.

After that disastrous lake vacation, when we arrived home, my parents announced that they had bought a lake house, in Vernon, N.J. I'm not sure how excited we were about that, after just getting home from spending a week in a gloomy, moldy, smelly, bug infested lake house, (shack).

It turned out the lake house my parents bought, was a real lake house. It was beautiful. You could sleep at least fifteen people in it. It was built on the lake's most beautiful location. The lake was man-made and the developer of the lake community built this house. The land came out like a little peninsula, and we had an enviable view of the lake. Our property was approximately five glorious acres of lake front property. It was truly a piece of Heaven, and as the kids grew up we spent many happy days in the spring and summer swimming, tubing, sailing, rowing, paddle boating, and inviting friends to enjoy what we had been blessed with. In the winter time, all the skiers in the family would go skiing at a nearby resort, located off of "Break Neck" road. Indeed the name of the road described it perfectly. It was a quarter of a mile with an incredibly deep slope. After a day of skiing, the tired athletes would come back to the house as Mom was making a pot of meatballs, and a roaring fire was snapping in the large stone living room fireplace. These were some of the best times.

We enjoyed Mom and Dad's lake house for approximately twenty-three years. We had to sell it after Mom passed away, because it would have been too much of a financial burden. After all those years, my brother and sister lost interest, and Jeff and I couldn't manage to maintain it. I am so blessed to have such great memories, but it still breaks my heart today that it's not ours anymore, especially knowing Mom wanted it to be in the family for generations to come. Unfortunately, her vision couldn't have been ours, too.

As a family we spent many mini vacations visiting my husband's parents Nana and Grampy Drown, in Massachusetts, where Jeff grew up and I attended college. Nana and Grampy loved our children so much and it was always great to spend time with them. It became more difficult as the kids grew up and were involved with sports, so unfortunately our trips became fewer as the years went by.

My father-in-law David, was a wonderful man, and was taken away from us much too soon. At sixty-four years old, he died of a massive heart attack. This happened even before Megan was born.

Phylis, my mother-in-law, managed to thrive and live alone, for about the next twenty years or so, before she succumbed to serious health issues and went to be with the Lord. She was always concerned about me. I would spend many hours talking to her about raising children, my Parkinson's, being a wife, getting older, and you name it. She was an incredibly wise and faithful woman of strength. She was always on my side when Jeff and I had our little disagreements. She loved me like a daughter. I miss her so much. She was a great mother-in-law, and I can honestly say that I loved her very much as well. At her funeral my sister in-law, Gail, and I found ourselves walking up to the grave and without a signal we both started wailing at the top of our lungs in sorrow. It was so strange. Everyone lifted their heads to look at this bizarre behavior. I just know it came from deep within, to express how we were so sad that we would have to be apart from this wonderful woman for so long. Gail and I looked at each other when we returned to the circle with this dumbfounded look on our faces. It was a testament to how much her daughters-in-law loved her.

Jeff's brother and sister and their spouses and children still live in Massachusetts, and we visit about once a year now. Traveling in the car is not always too comfortable for me, but I try to grit my teeth and bear it. Plus when we stay with people, now certain requirements have come into play. I need a bathroom on the same level. Sometimes it's difficult navigating at night. I also need to be able to say "no" to some of the activities that are being offered. It can be overwhelming as sometimes things are more difficult than others. Our family members are great, and they respect the fact that I'm not always up to par.

Cherry, Jeff's sister, and her husband, Sid, and Bill, Jeff's younger brother, and his wife Lisa, are so gracious when we visit. Cherry cooks the most wonderful gourmet meals. I love sitting at her kitchen island on a stool, and talking to her and watching her as she puts together her most fabulous, palate pleasing meals. She is a retired registered nurse, and has a lot of good advice, and information.

Lisa and Bill are fantastic. What I love about Lisa is that she is so nonchalant about my PD. She is a "Let's get the job done," kind of person. You do what you have to do and move on. She doesn't bug me. She puts it out straight, "Look if you need anything, or you don't feel right, just do what you have to do. If you need me, I'm here." I love that. She makes me feel normal. When I feel like crap, she doesn't hound me or offer solutions, like other people do when they know nothing about how to even begin to try to help me. Everyone is different, but with me, you just have to leave me alone, until I ask…..sorry, folks, that's just how it is. It is what keeps me grounded.

I have known Jeff's younger brother Bill, since I was in college. He was thirteen when we met. He has always been so dear to me. He is a man with a quiet gentle, spirit. He doesn't say much to me about PD, but his presence is one of protection, but not overbearing. He still treats me like one of his big sisters. They have one child, Rebecca, who has grown into the most beautiful, intelligent articulate woman, and is attending college. I love spending time with all of them.

Jeff's brother David, and his wife Gail, now live in Texas They have recently retired, and we've been able to spend more time with them, as they make their way back east every summer to early autumn. I like the "retired" David. He is so relaxed and so much fun. He just seems different. When

David laughs it makes me laugh. He has this hi-pitched almost ladies laugh, or like a rooster with a high voice clucking away. I laugh at him laughing. When we are in a restaurant, everyone turns their heads to our table to see who is making that crazy sound. I just laugh uncontrollably. Laughter is really good for what ails you, especially Parkinson's. We should all laugh more often.

Gail is a very intelligent, strong, take charge, kind of woman, yet very soft and gentle on the inside. I think we have grown much closer over recent years, as we share the good times as well as the times of grieving together and getting older together. They also have three children, Emily, Daniel, his wife Stacey, and Tyler. Emily and Dan live in Texas, and Tyler lives in New York City.

A few years ago, we were visiting Dave and Gail in Corpus Christi, Texas. We took a trip to San Antonio along with nephew, Tyler, to visit the Alamo, and do the River Walk. The River Walk is a lovely walk along the river, and it can be quite long, especially for a PLWP. I think this must have been the first time Gail and Dave really saw me totally "clicked off."

I don't think they fully understood how I couldn't put one foot in front of the other, but I kept trying. It's hard for someone to imagine what that feels like. Jeff can get testy with people at these times when they try to push me. But what ended up happening is that they kind of, hoisted me up by my elbows with my feet barely touching the ground and I more or less glided through the river walk. I can't imagine what this looked like. It brings a smile to my face. At the time, however, I thought to myself, "Why do I even try to go anywhere?"

The time came when Gail and I had to use the ladies room. I didn't know how I was going to do that because I was still pathetically "clicked off." Well, Gail somehow got me in there and noticed people staring at me. She shouted at them in a loud stern, controlled voice,

"PARKINSON'S!!"

I think that I "clicked in" right after that. I don't remember if I felt embarrassed, or thought, "Yea, that's right. It's Parkinson's!! You can stop staring, now, ladies."

Somehow I have digressed off our family activities and vacations. I am sharing stories as I come to remember them.

We took other vacations to different places like Myrtle Beach, S.C., The Outer Banks of North Carolina, and our favorite, when the kids were really young; camping either in Pennsylvania, or at the New Jersey shore.

Some of these trips were more memorable than others. We used to go camping with large groups of friends, mostly from our church family.

There was the time that we went to Lancaster, Pa. with a group of at least forty people, kids included. I have a strange feeling that this was before my diagnosis, or maybe at the very earliest beginning of my symptoms. It is hard to pinpoint. We have photographs of me with Megan in a sort of backpack on my back. That doesn't sound right. It was a kind of back pack for a person to carry a toddler in. This camp site was high up on a hill and required walking up this rocky road. We all pitched our tents at adjoining camp sites and I remember this trip as being one of the highlights of our family vacations. It was fun being with all those friends. We would wake up to the smell of cooking bacon and pancakes. Our friend, Joe, always loved making breakfast. Those were huge breakfasts for all the families.

During the day we toured the beautiful unspoiled farmland of the Amish countryside. We went on a tour of an actual working Amish farm. I was in awe over the complicated simplicity of the lives of the Amish people. I know that sounds strange "complicated simplicity," but these farmers and their families work so hard to not pollute the land, and to treat it with such respect and reverence. They don't use electricity, or any type of man-made power that involves destroying the earth. It looks so beautiful from the outsider's stand point, but an incredible amount of work. They don't take any more from the land than what they need, and they always replace it. It is a beautiful concept, but way beyond anything I could ever live by…. unfortunately.

At night we would come back to the camp sites and all get together around a roaring campfire and sing songs and tell crazy, sometimes scary stories. The kids would sing their special camp songs. Of course, we would have S'mores, too.

After several hours, the fire would die down and the kids, well more like the adults, would get sleepy, and we would all make our way to the out houses to use the bathroom one last time and brush our teeth, etc.

One particular night I was in charge of putting toothpaste on the toothbrushes of several children. It was really dark so I grabbed from my toiletry bag what I thought was a tube of toothpaste and spread the contents on one of the boy's toothbrushes. When he came back from the outhouse, he said, "Aunt Ruth, this toothpaste doesn't taste right." I got out my flash light, shined it on the tube and to my horror, realized that I had put "Preparation H", a hemorrhoid cream, on his toothbrush. The entire group of 40 people, roared with laughter. None of us will ever forget this. By the way, he spit it out so he never got sick from it. Thank goodness. Our kids are grown now, but they all remember every detail of this incident. Leave it to me to make a "memory."

I am blessed to have so many fond memories spent with family and friends. I won't bore the reader with all the funny, endearing details of each trip and each memory. I just want you to know that even struggling on a daily basis, I put on my game face, trusted in God, and did the best I could. It was not easy. I don't want it to appear that it was easy, but it can be done. A person has to find their own balance. It takes a lot of hard work. The balance comes from the medication, taking care of oneself, relationship to doctors, family support, and everyone being honest with each other. The latter being the most difficult, because it has taken me on a two decade journey to finally become honest with myself and those I love. I guess it worked for a while, I say with a little smile.

During these formative years of our family, to earn extra money, I gave piano lessons at home. Music was always flowing out of our windows in the spring and summer. I loved doing this because it allowed me to be at home with my children as they were growing up. Even though, to this day, they insist that they had come to hate the sound of the piano and me counting, "1, 2, 3, 4," and snapping my fingers to the beat of the music. I guess this must have been annoying, but hey, I was there for them. When the boys would be outside playing street hockey, I was the only mom home who would wipe the blood off of them.

I was also there to share the funny, and at the time, not so funny moments. They become hysterically funny as years go by.

One memory I have about the kids is when they were younger. I had had PD for several years. This incident still gives me a huge belly laugh as I remember it. I was teaching a piano student, and Megan and her little friend, Jaime, decided it would be really fun to spread soft soap on the floor of the girls' hardwood bedroom floor. Keep in mind their bedroom is 12 x 12 feet in area. I heard the girls laughing with such joy and delight. I commented to my piano student, "Wow, it sounds like they are really having fun up there."

It gave me pleasure just to hear them laugh. I should have known better. Well, the laughter continued and became louder and more hysterical. I decided I had better go and see what was going on. The two little girls were sliding from one end of the room to the other on soft soap that was spread all over the floor! Bubbles were everywhere. Included in this decadent behavior, was older sister, Elizabeth, who, should have known better. At the time, I couldn't see the humor in this, because the soap and bubbles were everywhere! How was I going to clean this up? All I could say was, "What the ___ (bleep) are you doing?" The girls were shocked at my choice of words. I'll never forget the look on their faces. I don't know who the most shocked was that day. We had a heck of a time cleaning that mess up. As you know, when you add more water to soft soap, it keeps making more bubbles.

The following pages contain memoirs that I put together. They were written as they happened. Each one represents a specific day as noted on each page. The feelings I have expressed, broke my heart all over again as after many years, I came back to finishing up my journey which I hope will become my book. By re-visiting these pages, I certainly realize how far I have come within myself, my resolve, acceptance, and coping with this disease, and somehow moving forward, even though the disease continues to rob me of the simplest of tasks on a daily basis.

Journal Memoirs

August 12, 2011

I can't stop crying. I'm tired of feeling this way. I woke up after a night of body racking dyskinesia. My writing is so small I can hardly read it. I hardly even have the strength to write. I am shaking from head to toe. I almost want to die. I feel really depressed. I can't walk and my mind is so cloudy. My head hurts. Maybe I am just losing my mind. I cry out to God, "Please make this go away I just want to be normal again. I feel so helpless, lost, and trapped inside my body that won't work. I wonder if this is the beginning of the end. Will I ever "click- on" again?"

I hear on the radio that it is a beautiful summer day. I look out the window and the sun is too bright. It hurts my eyes. I can barely breathe. My chest feels so heavy. Who can I call? I don't want to upset my family. I look at their photos all around the living room as I wait to "click on." As I continue to sit and wait, I see the faces of my children, wedding photos, graduation from college photos, my beautiful grandson, my parents, my husband and I. I love them all so much. They stare at me and the joy on their happy faces almost haunts me and breaks my heart. I can't let them see me like this because I am Mom, strong, independent, beautiful, (to them), funny, loving, and faithful. But now I feel like nothing. As the tears pour down I think of what is to become of me. Is this what depression feels like? Yet this is the real me. The Parkinson's me. The other, me is when my meds are working. That's a strange way to see myself. The thought occurs to me that the real me is the person I am when my medications are not working. It's so sad yet it is my reality. I am dependent on my medication and I hate that.

I digress now to before I clicked off today. I got up late (9:00) because today is Friday, and it's my day off. I went outside, watered my flowers, took a shower, got dressed, and boom! That's when my meds stopped working. That was three hours ago. This is what is known as "dosage failure."

I look around the house from my perch on the couch. I can sit up. Wow! The house is a mess. Usually I clean on Fridays, but today the bed is unmade, and the laundry is on the floor next to the washing machine. The vacuum sits idly as the dog hairs continue to multiply. I pick up my pen to write because I had an amazing thought, but now I forget what it was. Oh well. That's really funny. That's PD for you.

Right now, everything overwhelms me. I am hungry, but don't feel like eating. Thank goodness I didn't have any plans for today. It is days like this that I wonder how I get up and go to work on the other four days. I guess we do what we have to do.

As I continue to wait to "click on," I wonder why it is so bright outside. I feel like putting on sunglasses and putting down all the window shades. This doesn't sound like me. I love the sun, but today I feel nauseous. I would really like to sit outside and wait for butterflies and a hummingbird that visits my garden, but my legs feel like mush. I'm sure I couldn't make it out to the garden. It seems like a million miles away. I could crawl, but I find that rather humiliating. Besides, what would the neighbors think? I have crawled as a last resort at times. I wonder, "Why it is that I can crawl but not walk?"

It is now 2:00 pm. Four hours later. I still don't feel any relief. Where is the dopamine? At this point I can hardly write. I wish there was a PD hotline for people who feel this way. I long for some company, but wouldn't know what to do if someone came. I just need to be patient as I wait for relief.

My poor dog, Roxy, a beautiful Chocolate Labrador Retriever has been lying on the floor next to me all day. What a faithful companion. She is the best. I keep reassuring her that everything is ok. That this too shall pass. I will feed her and let her out soon. She looks at me with her sad brown eyes. If only she could talk to me; although, through her eyes, she does.

I would like to play the piano, but I would have to go upstairs to get my glasses, and that is way too far to try to walk to. Oh well, I guess I will have to try to take more meds.

Time is going by and I am getting more impatient. Am I somehow doing this to myself? I try to relax, but nothing is working. I really don't know why.

One thing PD has taught me is to be patient even when it is so difficult.

I think it has even made me a better person. I am not thanking the disease though. It is not a nice thing. It's God that is using PD to mold me into someone He wants me to be.

I wonder if anyone knows how important dopamine is. It is like the "Holy Grail" of movement. I am so jealous of people who can move without giving it a thought. "Why can't science figure this out? It seems it should have by now."

Today I am sick of the word "Parkinson's." It is just a name, but it is not who I am. Yet today it has consumed me.

At 7:00 p m after almost a whole day of being "clicked off," my right foot begins to wiggle. This is the first sign that my meds are working. Then my legs start moving and squirming. Pretty soon I can't sit still. I can finally get up and do something. Now the only problem is that I've taken too much medication and my dyskinesia are so bad. Somehow I manage to endure the dyskinesia dance and I make dinner for Jeff and me. Tonight it's only ham and cheese sandwiches but he won't mind.

Although Jeff has never said this to me, you can imagine how difficult it must be to live with a spouse that has PD. I know it breaks his heart as he watches me stumble about, and then observe my frenzied dyskinesia movements. Yet it never ceases to amaze me that he still loves me in spite of myself and what I have become. This is what true love is.

August 13, 2011

It's strange but if you saw photographs of me you would probably think that I am a pretty youthful, fifty-eight year old. I color my hair so that it still looks like my natural medium brown. At least that's what the hair color package says. I really try to take care of myself. This may sound really bad, but my vanity is another thing that keeps me going. I take care of my skin and hair. I Put my make-up on every day, do yoga, and exercise pretty faithfully. I walk about three to four days a week. It makes me feel better overall. It doesn't really do much for the loss of dopamine, but it probably helps other brain chemicals.

I weigh about twenty-five pounds less than I used to weigh before PD. So people who know me think I look so much younger now. I am actually in better shape than I ever was before. This must sound strange, but I work really hard at this.

There is actually nothing wrong with my muscles. It's just the connection of them to my brain that's in error. That is why I look good in photos and not videos. Photos hide my dyskinesia and PD symptoms, except for that infamous PD mask when I am photographed unaware and I can't quickly flash my photo smile. All Parkinsonians have that PD mask. It's like a frozen face. You can see it in the eyes. I never really thought I had it but people close to me see it when I am "clicked off". I still think I am full of facial expression in my mind, but then I look in the mirror and reality kicks in and I get it. I see what they are talking about.

October 15, 2011

Today I draw upon my faith to keep me going. I know Parkinson's is only temporary. I believe in a place called "Heaven." Someday I will have a new body.

I am resolved not to be ashamed anymore and to resign myself to the fact that I still have the ability to help others and share my faith with them. This doesn't mean that I don't have my bad days. Unfortunately, this disease not only affects your body, but your mind. I see little glimpses of forgetfulness, a little confusion at times, exhaustion, as well as sleeplessness and bad or unusual and sometimes disturbing dreams, bouts of depression, (only a few) and anxiety.

These periods of depression and anxiety are not at all frequent, but I have to be aware of them. The good news is that even though someday Parkinson's may take my mind and body, it will not take my spirit, because thankfully, that belongs to Jesus.

I have not lost my voice, drooled, nor do I have difficulty swallowing. I have no resting hand tremors to speak of, and no dementia. I read that most of these symptoms may be inevitable. I don't know what the future is for me, nor do I want to know. I can only hope and pray that a cure will come first. I function at a pretty good level most days. According to my neurologists and doctors I have already defied the odds. The progression of the disease is really slow. They have mentioned a new word, "Idiopathic Parkinson's." I don't even know what that means. So, I looked up "idiopathic" in the dictionary. It says that it is a disease of unknown etiology. Then I had to look up "etiology" just to be sure. It means "origin." That is just what I thought. It's also a fact that I already know. I have a disease of unknown origin. Anyway, I think my slow progression is partly due to my stubbornness, and defiance of this disease. It is mostly due to the fact that God is in control and I know people are praying for me. I can feel it.

I have heard some PLWPs say that PD has been a blessing to them. They have actually developed artistic creativity, and some artists have said that PD has changed their painting styles in positive and unique ways. Others have said that it has helped them appreciate and love their families more. That is truly wonderful to me. If I had to think of a positive aspect of PD, it would be that I have had to depend on God more. When I am frightened of falling or am awakened by nightmares, I call out to Him and He helps me put one foot in front of the other. Again, I know He is changing me to actually be better spiritual

June 3, 2012

I want to get up to read a passage in my Bible to inspire me. But all I can do is sit here and stare at the dining room table and shake. I am frozen, again. I can barely write. I just want to click in. I took ½ a pill an hour ago. I am impatient. So I take another ½ hoping for relief. I want to get moving. It's a beautiful day, but I can't move. If I try to, I will stumble. It's so hard to be patient. "Why is it taking so long?" My mind wants to begin the day, but my body doesn't. I cry alone, while Jeff sleeps. I woke up early thinking that I would click in. Sometimes I feel as if I am taking fake pills. It takes longer and longer to click in lately. I really need to join a support group. Does anyone know what I am going through? My family sees parts of it but I try to put on a good show for them. No one knows how sad I feel today. I just want to be normal.

I am tired of the stares when I have dyskinesia. They stare when I can't walk. They constantly and unabashedly stare. It's so hard. I have to fight to move. Somehow today I don't have the strength. Yesterday I got up early and felt good. Today I just don't know what is wrong. I have to focus and maybe my body will respond.

I am hungry. I want to put a piece of toast in the toaster oven, but even my small kitchen is too far away to get to. Now I have to go to the bathroom, but that is really too far away. I get down on my hands and knees and partly crawl to get there. How far down my life has gone? But not to worry, as soon as the dopamine kicks in all these feelings will disappear. I will be normal (sort of), again. My hand writing will become large, smooth, and flowing. I will get up, make my toast, go to the bathroom, and I will greet the day with joy and happiness once again. But I'm not there yet today. However, just the thought of freedom of movement inspires me not to completely shut down. I can't help wondering, however, if the time will come when my medicine no longer works. I pray with all my heart that God won't let me go there, at least not today.

When I write about how depressed I feel, you may wonder if I have ever had thoughts of suicide. I have not. I know the depression will fade away like the sun burns away the fog in the morning. I have too much to live for. I love life so much. God has blessed me with such wonderful children. They are my heart, joy, and heroes. They are everything to me. My husband is such a good man. I don't deserve him. I do not want to be a burden on any of them. I want to live because they love me. Even if they are embarrassed by me at times, they don't show it. They always want to help me, but there isn't much they can do. Walk for me? Carry me? They often ask, "Are you ok mom?" "Yes, I'm fine." is my usual answer. I don't want to worry them.

June 2012

Without dopamine, I am nothing. Without Jesus, I am less than nothing. What dopamine does for my brain is what Jesus does for my soul and spirit. I want to replace my dopamine with God. That would work! The reality is that He is allowing me to have Parkinson's to fulfill a bigger purpose in my life. I am counting on that. I don't have the answer yet, but I know someday all of my questions will be answered.

Right now I thank God for the medicine and the research that is being done to find a cure or just even ease the symptoms of the disease. Believe me I do not take this for granted for one minute. Of course I wish that I didn't have to take meds, but I am so glad that I still respond to them so well in spite of the side effects.

Today is not a bad day. I continue my journey and pray for His blessing and forgiveness for my feelings of desperation at times. I am happy today, because I can move.

June 25, 2012

Today, I am already late for work. I don't think I can do this today. For some unexplained reason, my meds are failing me. Whenever this happens, and it's not very often, at least not this severe, my sub-conscious, or maybe God tells me to write in my journal. When I feel good, there are days, weeks, even months that I don't write anything. It's times like these that I write. So I've decided to do just that.

I can't go to work if I can't walk and shake all over. It's going to be one of those days. I woke up at 2:30 am, after going to bed at 11:30. I Tossed and turned and had fretful nightmares. Again, I can't explain why my meds aren't working.

Maybe the reason is that I had a really busy weekend. I have to realize that I am not superwoman. The weekend left me exhausted, and not sleeping does a real job on me.

I hate letting people down. I try so hard to be normal. Sometimes I just have to give in to it. It overwhelms me and I stop fighting for a day. Today is that day. Somehow I will manage to do the laundry and change the bed sheets. I may have to hop or crawl. Lovely, isn't it? It is just another day in the life of a Parkinsonian.

My mind games aren't working today. It is probably because I am so tired. Hot weather and a lot of activity can dehydrate me. When I have dyskinesia I move around and sweat a lot. I guess I'm really not going to work today. This has only happened once or twice in the eighteen years I have been teaching ESL. I have great co-workers. They love and accept me with my PD.

My co-worker just texted me and said to sit back, relax, and feel better. She has my class. I couldn't ask for better people to work with.

Sometime in 2013

It is now about twenty-two years later, and I can honestly tell you that the feelings of hurt are completely gone. Because of God's faithfulness and love, I can say he hasn't abandoned me, but He walks alongside of me day by day. Some days are not great. I'd be a liar if I said I'm never frustrated or upset or depressed. It goes with the territory. You will see as I continue my journey on the following pages. Strange as it may seem, I feel the love of God stronger as He continues to mold my spirit into something greater than it was in 1989 when my strange symptoms began. I didn't know then that I would be able to even share my story twenty-five or more years later. Even when I feel as if I am at my wit's end, don't know what to do, am physically helpless, and out of control literally in my own body, He comes to me, comforts me, teaches me, and even gives me something to do. After two decades, I realize that at these times that I am in God's hands, and there is a greater purpose for my suffering.

The next section of my journey consists of larger chronological periods of time. Forgive me if some things are repetitious. I address each block of time as I remember it. Naturally I haven't shared everything, just what I feel is beneficial and trying to be as honest as I can be about my life as it was interrupted so cruelly now almost twenty-five years ago!

The First Five Years

For the first five years I was pretty good at masking or hiding my symptoms and condition. I was on a good regime of medication that seemed to work very well for me. I actually looked and felt pretty normal. During this period, I went back to work as a substitute teacher in the elementary and middle schools in our town, and I continued teaching piano. After about two years, I obtained a job as an ESL instructor at the local community college. Things were going pretty well. I was still for the most part hiding my affliction. I learned many tricks or gimmicks to mask my symptoms because they were still mild enough and the drug cocktail was doing its job. But that was about to change.

As insidiously as my Parkinson's symptoms began, so did the side effects of the drug "Sinemet." It started in my right foot. It just started twisting a little when I would be using it. It didn't feel bad; in fact, it felt good. It was better than the trembling and slowing down of movement that I was experiencing when my medicine "clicked off." That is how I describe it when my dosage wears off and I need more dopamine. Almost all PLWPs come up with that term by themselves, and then realize that everyone else also uses it. It's really weird. I thought I invented the term, but read it in Michael J. Fox's book, "Lucky Man." The reason why we say "I'm clicked on or off" is because it happens so quickly sometimes, like a light switch being turned on or off. The daily fluctuations are constant, and every day is like riding a roller coaster. I'm "on" I'm "off," etc. It can be nerve racking and exhausting.

These little squirming movements in my foot gradually became much more dramatic and began to involve my whole leg, other foot and leg, and eventually my whole body. These movements are called dyskinesia and are physically draining. Sometimes my muscles ache from them.

As my side effects from the medicine worsened, my neurologist put me on various other meds to counteract the side effects from the Sinemet. Some of them had nasty side effects of their own. One particular drug really helped my PD symptoms, but kept me awake all night and when I would fall asleep for a few seconds I would have violent nightmares. I thought I would lose my mind, so I had to get off of that drug. So far, I have only mentioned the name of one drug and that is Sinemet. Everyone knows that this is the premier drug therapy for PD.

I feel that each person who manages living with PD should discover their own therapies with their doctors. Privately I will tell anyone anything about my disease and treatment. Needless to say, I have tried just about everything under the sun as far as medication goes. My physicians and I make changes together to come up with what works for me.

Since the very onset of PD in my life, my doctors have been great about listening to what I have to say. I am pretty good at knowing what works for me and what doesn't. I am very vocal in telling them how I feel. They have pretty much let me decide when to take my meds. I am very sensitive to what is going on in my body, and I have learned to time it as well as I can. I realized that I could no longer take the whole Sinemet pill because I am so sensitive to it and will have such severe dyskinesia. I discovered by taking one half, or one third of a pill, I could cut down on the involuntary movements, or dyskinesia. I would always have a pill or two in my pocket, and break it into pieces. I would have to take it more frequently, but it seemed to smooth out the side effects and I could feel more normal for a longer period. Of course it is very difficult to deal with brain chemistry, because it is always changing and affected by many things, including hormones, diet, etc., but we do the best we can

*B*eyond the First Five Years

Beyond the First Five Years
Obviously it became more apparent to everyone around me that something was wrong with me. I started filling in people and officially came out of the Parkinson's secret "closet." I don't know why we Parkinsonians try to hide this disease for so long. For me it was the embarrassment. It's really so much better when people know, then they don't wonder why I do what I do with my body. My time for "coming out" was exactly the same time as Michael J. Fox. It was thrilling for me. Now this ridiculous, "old people" disease that I had actually had a face, a young, famous face! People would know what I was talking about when I said, "I have Parkinson's disease." They usually responded, "Oh yeah, like Michael J. Fox."

I will forever be grateful to Michael for not being ashamed like I was, and teaching us all that you can still live, thrive, and work even with a debilitating brain disease, not to mention any other disease that causes a person to withdraw. The research that The Michael J. Fox Foundation does in Parkinson's is beyond comparison. I do believe there will be a cure in the not so distant future. He has totally inspired me. He has to be one of my heroes. His passion for the Parkinson's community is contagious. I wish I could meet Michael, but I already feel as if I know him. We share many of the same symptoms and side effects of medication.

$\mathcal{T}$he Next Decade

Since the time my dyskinesia became worse, it was obvious that I couldn't hide my PD anymore. I continued telling people. Most of the time, the response was shock and feeling sorry for me, which I hated. After all, I was still the same person, and yet in some sense I was a whole lot different. I wanted to be my old self, but somehow a new self was making its way out. I'm not saying that this was even a bad thing. It might have made me even a better person. I know this sounds really ridiculous, and it is hard to explain. I became freer as I shared my story with others and now they looked at me differently, but not in a negative way anymore. People were interested in my disease, treatment, and how I coped with it. I began to wonder if maybe I could use this disease to help, encourage, and comfort others, not only PLWPS but people who suffer for any reason.

It was around this time that I started to participate in The Parkinson's "Unity Walk" in New York City's Central Park. Encouraged by my family and friends, who promised they would walk with me, I proceeded to set up my team "Drowning PD". We started our participation in 2007. I have only missed two years since then. In the first three years of participation, my team raised over $17,000.00. I will continue to participate in the future. People have been so kind and generous.

At the "Unity Walk" I marvel over the love and sense of community that surrounds all of us. Amongst the hard realities of PD, there is so much joy present on this day. It's almost a celebration of those who are living with PD. They happen to be some of the most wonderful people, who don't deserve this monster yet, all of us are so loved by the people around us. You can see it in the faces of all the teams and their members, as well as the volunteers who so selflessly donate their time and energy to this wonderful worthy cause. We owe them all a debt of gratitude and thanks.

The Unity Walk is a time to share stories, strategies, meet people, and gather new information from the rows of booths containing doctors, pharmaceutical representatives, and various others. The whole day is inspirational. In the past five years I have heard speakers such as Michael J. Fox, Janet Reno, Davis Phinney, and Mohammed Ali's daughter, Mai, Mai, and many others.

Thank you to great doctors, changing therapeutic techniques, walking, exercise, yoga, staying active, and having the constant support of my family and friends who see me, not the disease, I actually feel better than I did twenty years ago. I don't know how that is possible, other than perhaps a miracle and trusting in God to carry me through each day, as I prayerfully submit to Him.

I am not saying that I don't have really bad times when nothing works, and I am depressed, desperate, frozen, and shaky, but I always keep in mind that another day will come and I will feel better. I also realize that I have a debilitating, degenerate brain disease that is progressive. I still don't know what my future holds. But, I can be grateful for today and thank God that the prognosis was wrong about being in a wheelchair in five years.

My story was featured in the Unity walk Hall of fame as a "Shining Star" in Sept. of 2012. I am by no means a "Shining Star." I am just a person dealing with and managing a disease. The Shining Stars are the PLWPs who are in advanced stages of PD and their caregivers. I feel their pain, and while I still have the ability to put one foot in front of the other, I will participate in the Unity Walk, and continue to raise funds for Parkinson's research. This is what the Unity Walk is all about.

Keeping a Sense of Humor

As my dyskinesia worsened, which I can never believe that it can continue to worsen and become so ridiculous, I would like to relate some rather annoying aspects of what it is like living with symptoms of PD and drug side effects.

People are always staring at me, especially my legs and feet. Not because they are glamorously beautiful, but because they never stop moving. After I take a good dose Carbidopa/levodopa, my feet dance all over the place, and if I'm standing too close you may get a swift kick that I usually don't mean to give you. After a while my whole body begins to squirm. I fight the impulses so hard that it is painful and sometimes I just have to go with them. It's a struggle.

I know people mean well, but some of the comments I have received are rather amusing. That is where a positive attitude and a sense of humor come in handy. Because part of me wants to just scream out, "Are you stupid or something?" Like when people ask me if I have to go to the bathroom. Really, I am a grown woman do you think I would be moving like this if I had to go to the bathroom? If I had to go, I'd go. I wouldn't stand here squirming. I still hear this comment on a weekly basis when I am checking out at a store. It drives me nuts! Another good one is, "Do you know your foot (leg) is moving?" Duh, like I can't feel my leg swinging from side to side. I'm not in a coma.

Another favorite was a comment a man said while I was waiting in line at a deli counter. "Are you a dancer?" He asked. My response was not so pleasant this time.

"NO!! I have Parkinson's Disease!" Usually I take the time to explain.

I just wasn't in the mood on this particular day. So the nice man just said, "I'm so sorry." I responded, "That's ok it's not your fault."

Then there was the time in a random ladies room that a woman clearly staring wide-eyed at my legs and feet belted out **"SAY WHAT?"** I didn't say, **"WHAT,"** or anything back to her.

Another funny observation I made a few years ago involved one of my ESL classes. As I mentioned before, my students are wonderful and really treat me with respect, and sometimes they imitate me. I am very important to them as they try to learn their second language, English. It's almost as if I am the key to their success. I usually have a desk in the front of the room, and my class always gives me their undivided attention.

I have a tendency to swing my right foot around as I also move my leg back and forth. I just happened to notice that almost all of the women in my class were doing the same thing. It was really funny. I guess they were unconsciously imitating my movement, as they were trying to imitate my words, and command of the English language. I really can't explain it, but it really happened. Life is just full of these little amusements. You just have to keep your eyes open!

The next comment is my all-time favorite. It came when my daughter and I were in a department store at the mall. A saleswoman joyously burst out with, "Oh look at you! You have such "Happy Feet!"

Megan and I looked at each other and she said, "Oh yes mom, you do have happy feet!"

Now that was a positive way of describing my feet under the influence of L-Dopa and dyskinesia: "Happy Feet." Megan then had a striking thought and said, "Mom you should write a book and call it "My Happy Feet!"

$\mathcal{M}$y Job

My Job
My ESL students have always been wonderful, kind, and compassionate, accepting and generous people. Whenever I start a new class, one of the first things I tell them is that I have Parkinson's disease. I down play it and just say that I'm ok but if look a little strange or move about in an odd way, it's because of the disease and medication side-effects. Most of my students are immigrants from other countries. Others are students who are studying for their GED exam (General Education Diploma), really respond to me. I have developed close relationships with many of them who have expressed the fact that I have been an encouragement to them, because I continue to push forward with a handicap. Many of them have had to overcome very difficult situations such as discrimination, loss of jobs, substance abuse, physical abuse, language barriers and some very serious health issues as well. Not to mention the fact that they have left their homes, families, and countries to come to the U.S. to supposedly find a better life. Sometimes their expectations are raised so high. They have described their ideas or images of what they thought America looked like before they came. It's almost as if the streets were paved with gold, and everyone was rich. According to many standards we are rich, but these immigrants have had to work extremely hard to make it in this country. If I can affect a change for the positive my job is so worthwhile, and gives me such affirmation.

I have had situations at work when my co-workers and students had to go the extra mile for me. One time when I was "clicked off" and stuck sitting at my desk waiting for my meds to kick in after my class had left, my co-worker at the time, came in to check on me before she left. I don't even know why she checked on me this particular time. My normal time to leave is 2:00 p.m. This co-worker and friend literally sat there with me for about an hour. I'm sure she had better things to do. I will never forget her friendship and willingness to help me. She helped me on many occasions, to which I will always be grateful. I remember feeling bad that she was wasting her time. She responded with,

"Do you think I would leave you like this? I will stay with you as long as it takes." That, to me, is the epitome of friendship and compassion. She never told anyone, nor did she ever bring it up again. Others at work have helped me and sat with me on different occasions.

My students have always marveled at the energy that I have. For better or worse most of my energy, enthusiasm, and animation is because of the dopamine rush that is caused by my medication. It acts like a stimulant for me, and causes me to be extremely energetic, (including dyskinesia), which they usually come to accept very quickly. I think fast, and come up with humorous anecdotes. I am "on," and they love it. They have asked me where my energy comes from and I usually just shrug my shoulders not really wanting to get into it, depending on my mood.

They have also seen me in a sense tread water, as my dopamine levels decrease dramatically. When this happens I am not quick witted, amusing, or even very talkative. I tell them I am having difficulty with my meds and they compassionately say, "It is ok teacher, just relax." They work independently and come up to my desk if they need help. They are amazing and compassionate. This is another reason I love my job. I have found that people really are basically good and want to help.

My students have been so generous, showering me with gifts at Christmas, surprising me with all kinds of food, praying for me, and in return I give them whatever I can, but mostly just myself in bareness and all honesty. What you see is what you get.

I sometimes tend to beat myself up when I "click off" when I am with people. I know that it's not my fault, but I get mad that it happens. "Did I lose track of time and not take my medication because I was feeling good?" This happens. I get so caught up in teaching and feeling good that I unwittingly delay my next dose.

A normal person cannot understand how wonderful it feels to feel good. That is an ever fleeting feeling for me. One minute I'm "on" and the next, I'm "off," that constant roller coaster of feeling good versus bad. Not a great way to live, but as I say time and time again, "It is my reality, and if you are in my life, you better just hang on and roll with it."

$\mathcal{M}$ore Recent Changes

More Recent Changes

Moving on to about the end of the tenth year of living with Parkinson's, the next development in my progression, and is the worst for me, is something called "freezing." This was and continues to be the worst experience for me. It can be terrifying. Freezing is when for no apparent reason your feet and legs refuse to move. It's as if your feet are glued to the floor. You try to lunge forward but you know you will fall if there is nothing to fall into or hold on to. So in my case, I just stand there and sometimes move my feet up and down or from side to side to try to get going. Sometimes it is futile. This seems so ridiculously stupid to me and I get frustrated and angry at myself. I will try to talk to my brain to tell my feet to move. A person shouldn't have to tell their brain to move their feet. I keep thinking it's something I'm doing wrong, like I'm willing my feet not to move. But who would do that? Then I try playing games with my brain and sometimes this works. I take a deep breath and carefully and cautiously lift my legs as if I am stepping over something like a big log, or I will try to march like a soldier...fun, right? But I can actually get my brain into gear sometimes by accessing other areas of movement, like jumping, skipping, or hopping. I know this sounds weird but it works and is better than falling. I think after twenty-three years of living with PD, I have only gone down maybe once or twice.

A miracle of the human experience is that if the brain is working properly, and all connections between brain chemicals, nerves, and muscles are working smoothly, people just walk. They put one foot in front of the other and never think about it. Not so with people living with Parkinson's. Yet when the meds click in, I do walk without thinking about it. What a glorious feeling, until the dyskinesia literally, "kick" in.

To this day, freezing causes the most anxiety for me, and I deal with it on a daily basis. My days are like riding a roller coaster as I have mentioned before. I am "on," "off," "frozen," severe dyskinesia, and for a few fleeting moments, sometimes more on a great day, I actually feel **NORMAL**.

Another strange manifestation is that if I am in an open space, I can walk pretty smoothly, although slowly, with concentration, but still moving forward. If I am in small spaces, or a door frame, I begin to freeze. I can go up and down stairs normally even when "clicked off." I don't really know why. I think it may have something to do with gravity. Who knows?

I also love to swim. I spend many hours during the summer in my son's in ground pool. I think I am my grandson Nick's favorite "pool mate." One day we were in the pool for 3 hours straight. I literally looked like a huge prune. Nick has gotten me to do canon ball jumps into the water, hand stands, and more recently, he taught me how to use a snorkel and mask. We are ready to go Scuba diving. Oh, I also do somersaults in the water. Anything for Nick! We laugh hysterically when we look at each other in our diving masks underwater. The reason I love the water and pool so much is that it almost totally relieves my symptoms. I feel light, and smooth. I can swim so well, float, and just feel totally relaxed. I think if I was a mermaid, I wouldn't need medication. I could just live in the water. Thank goodness Nick loves the water too! The other three grandkids are much younger, but it looks like they are going to be fish also. I will always have someone to swim with!

To this day, I want to convince my brain that it is mind over matter, but unfortunately it won't cooperate with me. This causes a lot of frustration. But I am still convinced that somehow visualization, and trying to re-route your mind has something to it and I would somehow like to explore this. How? I have no idea. The brain is so powerful. There must be some way to sort of mentally stimulate other parts of the brain. I think we all would like to think about this.

June 2014

On a brighter note, I just have to write about how much I enjoy watching and taking photos of the sunrise, especially when it rises over the ocean at the New Jersey shore.

When we stay down the shore, I wake up early almost every day. If I can walk, or sometimes if I'm late, I run to the beach to witness this special gift of natural revelation. The fact that I can even walk or run is a revelation in itself.

I go by myself, because no one wants to get up. I always tell them that they have no idea what they are missing. Well, a few times my faithful husband has gone with me. Those times usually ended up being cloudy. He is always a good sport. Even the ominous dark clouds are hauntingly beautiful. They are another side of God's masterpiece of nature.

Every time I see the sunrise I think of God's faithfulness in letting it rise another day. It's like a promise. The night may be difficult, but the sun will come up and spread its light. It becomes so brilliant that I can't even look at it when it is completely revealed. It reminds me that the face of God has never fully been seen because it is so brilliant and bright.

"You cannot see my face, for man may not see me and live." Exodus 33:20

Every sunrise is different. I have thousands of pictures to prove this. I usually come back to the house, excited about my photos and I hear, "Yeah, yeah, Ruth, another sunrise." They all look the same!" No! You have to look at each photo to see the gradual progression…..hum does that sound familiar? I stake my life on gradual progression

August 2016

It has been a few years since I started writing about my journey with Parkinson's, but somehow the block has lifted. Perhaps because my husband and I just got back from a weekend with two of our dearest friends from college who managed to listen to me for two days, as I shared my experiences over the last decade and before. As I let loose of my feelings we laughed, cried, and I realized something. They still love me and accept me in spite of the crazy movements of dyskinesia, the FOG (failure of gait), and my obsession with my "little blue pills." In fact, I managed to give everyone a pill at some point, because my Jeggings "jean leggings" didn't have pockets, or I was in a bathing suit. Jeff carried a few in his wallet. My friend, Mari, carried a few in her pocket. I always have to make sure that they are available. I digress again! The point is, they saw me, not my PD and somehow they brought me back to writing my story. I hope they don't mind that I have started referring to them as my muses.

I think the reason that I was able to get back to writing my story about my journey with PD directly relates to the weekend that Jeff and I spent with Mari and Gary. I would like to add this "revelation" as part of my journey, because it made me realize that I have a voice and I have things to say, or write. Sometimes the things I have to say are heartbreaking. At best they may be even inspiring, but sometimes they are just funny, really funny as my friends made me realize.

After about eight years of not being able to write, the next part of my journey is written in present time, but deals with memories of the past

*W*riter's Block "Gone"

We arrived in New Hampshire, at Lake Winnipesaukee, on Saturday afternoon, spent the rest of the day touring the lake on Gary's boat, and catching up with news of the last ten years, or so. We talked about our children, grandchildren, our lives, health, jobs, hopes, dreams, and just simply laughing, crying, and reminiscing over the past, when we were young, poor, and physically fit, for the most part. We spoke about our prospects of retirement, and lastly our parents who except for two fathers, have departed this earth. Gary's dad just celebrated 101, and my dad who is in an Alzheimer's unit and is struggling along at 93 years old. We drank Gary's famous Margaritas, while watching the glorious sunset on the lake. Later on that evening we hugged, kissed, and said, "Good night." We looked forward to the coming day together even though we really didn't know exactly what we were going to do.

Sunday morning we woke up to a fairly cloudy day. The threat of rain was in the forecast. We all agreed it would be nice to go for a ride to the White Mountains and Franconia Notch. After breakfast we piled into the car and began our laugh filled journey.

After several hours we ended up at the beautiful, majestic Mount Washington Hotel. We took lots of photos, had lunch, and then set out for Franconia Notch and "The Old Man of the Mountain."

I am sure not everyone is familiar with "The Old Man of the Mountain" unless you are from New England, especially because it no longer really exists. It was a rock formation jutting out the side of a mountain that uncannily resembled a man's profile. To me it looked like Abraham Lincoln's profile. He no longer exists because due to erosion and the elements, he crumbled down the face of the mountain in May of 2003.

It is sad that the real profile is no longer there, but surprisingly enough there is still a way to see him. There is an area in the park that has many imprints of footprints in concrete. Each set of footprints has height measurements in them. It took us a while to figure it out because we were looking down at the footprints, wondering, "What the heck?" Here's the answer. If you stand in your approximate height measured footprint, and you look up, you will see "The Old Man of the Mountain!" It is quite amazing. There are artistic looking sculptures on steel rods. The way the exhibit works is that the rods and sculptures meet up with the individual's sight line and creates the perfect illusion. As you look up you see "The Old Man of the Mountain" in the exact spot that he was at. It is so amazing. It is almost better than the real thing! So the good news is "He's back!"

Before we got to the exhibit as I just mentioned, we approached the spot where we thought the profile was once proudly exhibited. My mind rushed back to another time years before, when as a child, I thought I saw his profile. The key word here is "thought." At the present time, the four of us adults, couldn't remember where it was, but we imagined where it had been. As a child I didn't know exactly what I was looking for, so I imagined it on every mountainside.

This brought me back to one of the many vacations that my dad took us on. We were a family of five; Mom, Dad, my older sister, Grace, me, and my younger brother, Bill. The first vacation I remember was our New England trip. This trip was the first of many excursions. Somehow, this mountain, and the memory of the profile I never really saw as a child, stirred up these memories so clearly and I started relating the stories of my family vacations with my dad as tour guide. My friends and Jeff, who may or may not have heard parts of these sagas before, listened attentively. Before long, we were all laughing hysterically and I couldn't stop as I related one story after the other of our vacation debacles. Finally, Gary said, "Ruth, you really should write these stories down because they are really funny."

I never realized other people would find them so amusing, so now I am going to try to share them.

Vacations with Dad

In thinking about my feelings as a child about our vacations, it has finally come to me. Our vacations consisted of us watching other people having fun on their vacations. It was as if we were spectators of others unabashedly and voluptuously enjoying themselves on vacations as they participated in whatever activities were available to that particular vacation spot. I know this may not sound like fun, but in a weird way it was for us. I really should speak for myself; it was fun for me. We were together and in a new place. I relate these stories with a sense of humor and complete love and appreciation for my parents who tried to show us different areas of the U.S.

As I continued to tell each vacation story, Gary realized the central figure controlling the dynamics of our vacations was my father. With his type "A" driven personality, Dad was the dynamic in making our vacations so funny, unique, and unforgettable.

My dad was an electrical engineer, who eventually owned his own business. He was driven to work through the night pouring over shop drawings in order to get the job done. He was smart, abrupt, sometimes rude, and even abrasive. He always had a plan. As a child and young man, he lived through poverty of the depression, alcoholic parents, abuse, and was a World War II veteran. As an adult he became driven and obsessed to provide for his family. His mind was always racing. Needless to say he was always working, except for family vacations.

I digress back to the "Old Man of the Mountain." As my family and I drove through the White Mountains in our tan Ford Falcon station wagon, we approached Franconia Notch and had our heads craned at the neck and our eyes straining as we looked at every mountain ledge, so we wouldn't miss the "Old Man." But Dad, being the way he was, didn't want to take the time to go to the visitor's information area. "Because, they just want to make money," He said. We could find it on our own. So, we just drove through the winding mountainous roads of the White Mountains saying, "There it is. I see it. No, there it is. I see it now. Oh no. There it is…for sure!" We saw him on the side of every mountain. We were so sure. It was so cool to go back home to New Jersey and talk about seeing "The Old man of the Mountain." But now I know we never really saw him. I am sure the people we saw at the visitor's center saw the real "Man of the Mountain." I finally did see him when I was in college in Massachusetts and my boyfriend, who is now my husband, took me to Franconia Notch and gave me the full tourist treatment, and I was introduced to the real "Man of the Mountain." I will be forever grateful.

On that same New England trip, on another day, we packed up our bags to move to the next hotel and went to Cape Cod, famous for its scenic coast. We came to the coast, and Dad parked the car on the side of the road. We walked onto the beach in our pants, shoes, and sweaters, and stood on some rocks for about five minutes. The ocean looked so beautiful and inviting to me. I had never been in it. The wind was blowing my hair, and the sun was beginning to lower in the sky. My adventurous brother chased after a few waves as they ebbed up onto the sand. I wanted to stay. Well, dad took a movie about three minutes long, and announced "Time to go. It's getting late."

As we walked to the car, I glanced back over my shoulder, to see people in their bathing suits still enjoying the water and the beach. I wondered what that would be like. I knew I wanted to experience it, but off the beach we walked as the orange and red sun continued to make its descent into the most beautiful sunset I have ever seen. How I longed to stay. Not surprisingly, chasing sunrises and sunsets became a passion of mine over the years so this longing continues to be fulfilled.

Perhaps the most memorable vacation was our trip to California, probably because it was the longest vacation we ever had. We roamed the coast of the Big Sur Highway for about a week. My dad rented a car in Los Angeles and we drove up the entire coast, again, passing by many famous attractions. The only attraction my mom mentioned was "Knott's berry farm." It was the only tourist attraction that she requested to see. I think she must have thought that it was a big farm where you could see animals and buy all sorts of jellies and jams. I have no idea where she even heard of it. To this day, I thought it was a farm, because we never made it to the "farm." As I was remembering this, I googled "Knott's berry farm," and discovered that it is not a farm but a huge amusement park. Oh my dear mother wanted to go to a farm.

The most eventful time we had on that vacation was at Disney Land. We actually got to do something. We were walking around the park for several hours looking for the shortest ride line, when Dad decided we were hungry. He heard a band playing music at one of the outside eateries under a tent. It sounded like John Phillips Sousa March music. The four of us sat down so we wouldn't lose our table while dad went to get five large milkshakes and burgers. As he walked back, he was carrying the tray on one hand held up in the air, like a very experienced waiter would do. The music was loudly playing with the horns blasting and the drums carrying on the beat of the march. Dad, who incidentally was a pretty serious guy most of the time, decided to do a little dance, or march. I'm not exactly sure what his awkward movements were meant to be, but for two split seconds, my family was greatly amused and excited that dad was having fun. That was about it, because after those two seconds, someone yelled out to him, "Show off!" With that, he lost his composure and down went all the milkshakes and burgers. I don't know what we salvaged out of that meal to eat. Dad was pissed! Thankfully, the scene did not end here but became a hysterical image that to this day is etched in my memory.

A few minutes later several groups of people came by not knowing what was on the ground, and they slipped and slid uncontrollably. No one could get traction on that slimy mess. It was unbelievably funny. You really had to be there. We pretended that we knew nothing about the mess, and became observers of this melee. This may not even sound funny, but to us it was, and the fact that dad was an active participant in keeping this secret as we could see him trying to control his laughter.

Did we go on any rides at Disney World? We went on the ride: "It's a Small, Small World." My mom thought it was the most wonderful thing she had ever seen. The words of that song still repeat in my mind, because I think we went on it three times that night. That was it. Our trip to Disney World was over. I don't even know if we stayed for the fireworks….oh well. I would see them someday with my husband and children.

The main purpose of this California trip was to drive up the gorgeous coast of California and drive on the Big Sur Highway as I mentioned previously. So, that is exactly what we did. I must say that I have beautiful images of the majesty and natural beauty of this drive. Our first destination was Pebble Beach. Pebble Beach is famous for golf. The hotel was fabulous and probably very expensive, however, no one played golf in my family, so another example of, "Well, it's really beautiful here, but what are we are supposed to do?" So we walked around, ate three meals, and went for another drive.

Perhaps the funniest memory I have is after we reached our next destination, San Francisco. San Francisco is such a beautiful, exciting city. Riding up and down those steep hills on cable cars was exhilarating. My brother, sister, and I couldn't get enough of it. The time came for us to check into our hotel room, which incidentally, was in one of the finest hotels in San Francisco back in the '60s. It was the Sir Francis Drake Hotel. I remember the name of it, because my dad kept saying it over and over again to impress us with how lucky we were to have the privilege of staying in a famous hotel.

My dad went to the front desk, got the keys to our adjoining rooms, and we proceeded up the elevator to our rooms. We were filled with anticipation of how they would look in this expensive, old, classic hotel. We all stood flanking my dad on all sides and staring at the door of the room. We couldn't wait to see what was inside. As he turned the key in the knob, the door opened a crack. We tried to look inside. As it opened wider and we all peered in, we were shocked to see a very tall, thin, mostly bald-headed man sitting on his chair in front of the T V eating his dinner on a tray. I say "tall" because it looked as if his knees were up to his chin. He was in his underwear and had a skinny tee-shirt on. The look on his face was a cross between astonishment, fear, anger, and most of all indignation. True to form, my dad said, "Excuse me, I'm sorry, but you are in my room. The man responded with something like,

"Clearly sir, this is my room, since I'm sitting here having dinner."

"No," Dad replied. "This is my room. You can see the number on the door matches my key."

Please keep in mind that we three kids were still staring at the poor guy. With that my mother, in her most reasonable voice said, "Come on Bill, I'm sure there's been some mistake. We can get another room." Ah, the voice of reason. I am sure Dad still felt that it was his room and the man should have gotten dressed and packed up and left. To this day, I can still see the look on that guy's face when some stranger and his family broke into his hotel room while he was relaxing and having dinner; what an invasion of privacy.

On that same trip to San Francisco, my parents, who rarely went out alone on a date, made reservations to a famous restaurant, Trader Vic's. They left the three of us alone. We were allowed to get room service for dinner. My sister and I were so excited about ordering the food and then eating it when it came; that we really didn't notice my little brother was missing. He had to be around seven years old. When we realized he really was nowhere in our hotel rooms, we started to panic. We really didn't know what to do. So we just sort of stood around looking at each other trying to figure out what to do. I felt that my sister, who was five years older than me should take charge. After all, she was the oldest. She just kept asking me what to do. What did I know? I was just a stupid little kid of about eleven years old. The next thing we know, my parents arrived and asked, "Where is Billy?"

Ah. Good question. Almost at the exact same moment, Bill came shooting through the door and in his hand was a caricature drawing of himself that an artist had drawn down at Fisherman's Wharf. Somehow the little bugger managed to take a cable car, went down to Fisherman's Wharf and hired an artist to draw a caricature of him. I don't know if he even had any money. We were extremely relieved that he was ok. In fact, he felt grown up, independent, and better than ever.

A few years later, we went on a vacation to the "Big Sky Country" which included Utah, Wyoming, Montana, and Idaho.

I'll begin with Utah. We visited the Mormon Tabernacle, heard the choir, went to the museum, and learned about Joseph Smith. I really wasn't too interested. I was just happy that my hair looked so good because of the dry weather! The event I was looking forward to was going to Salt Lake. I heard that you could float on top of the water so easily because of the salt. It sounded really cool. We drove around for as long as it takes to get from Salt Lake City to Salt Lake. I didn't think it would be a long trip, but it was for us. We never found Salt Lake. I don't quite understand why. Every time we saw a sign for Salt Lake, Dad would follow it and we would end up in the same place. We kept going in circles. I don't know what he was missing, but no one could figure out how to find the lake. We began to doubt that there actually was a Salt Lake. It certainly couldn't be very large if we couldn't even find it. So, after following signs for Salt Lake that didn't lead us to Salt Lake, we just continued on our journey. In reminiscing about Salt Lake, I discovered that not only is it big; it is huge! You can see it on a Google map from way up into the stratosphere

Our next stop was Jackson Hole, Wyoming. Jackson Hole is a famous ski resort. Even though it was early summer, believe it or not, there was snow on top of the mountains and people were skiing. Well, maybe not enough snow for skiing, but hiking. Of course, none of us had ever been hiking, or skiing so the highlight of that stay was playing with the two Saint Bernard dogs, Dinky, and Stinky. They even had those little barrels around their necks. Those dogs would be the closest I ever came to skiing or hiking at Jackson Hole. But it was fun to see all the good looking young people come in from the slopes with their cheeks all rosy from enjoying the mountains. Whatever it is that people do in the mountains, they looked so invigorated and happy.

The best time I had on that trip was horseback riding with Bill, at the "Lazy P" Ranch in Montana. I was a fairly experienced rider, since I had taken horseback riding lessons for several years. Bill, on the other hand, had never been on a horse. My parents just left us there and we got on our horses, and the horses took us off into wilderness of Montana. I loved it. I was actually a participant in my vacation! I was doing something. I was riding a horse in Montana. I was so happy to be on a horse that I kind of forgot about Bill, again. I was galloping, when I heard Bill screaming my name, "RUTH, RUTH **STOP!**"

I turned around and there was Bill riding the underbelly of the galloping horse. Sometimes horses fill up their lungs and expand when a saddle is put on. Then, when the horse relaxes, the saddle loosens around the horse's girth. It was priceless, but also a little scary. I certainly didn't want my little brother to get hurt. Somehow we managed to secure the saddle and even though I didn't know how to get back to the ranch, the horses knew where they were going and brought us back.

When we got back to the ranch, Mom and Dad were there waiting for us. They asked us if we had a good time. I said, "Yes it was fantastic!"

Bill said, "I hate horseback riding. Ruth wouldn't stop!"

The last event of that trip was our Jeep ride up the Grand Teton Mountains, or I should say, partially up the mountainside of the Grand Tetons. Dad was getting more adventurous on this trip and decided to rent a Jeep and go off-road. He had never driven a Jeep and really didn't know what "off road" meant.

I must say I think this is the most scared that I have ever been. We were on this extremely narrow dirt road and out the right hand of the jeep was a sheer cliff looking down into what looked like Death Valley. It seemed like it had a million foot drop. We knew if Dad couldn't keep on the path, we would be dead. My mother was screaming, "Bill let us out of the Jeep." He ignored her for a while, and then we all started screaming, "Dad…DAD!!!" Finally he got mad at us, of all things, and let us out. He continued to try to make his way up the mountains.

Well, at least we were participating in our vacation! My mom, my brother, and I walked down the side of the mountain and ended up at a beautiful, icy cold rapidly racing stream that was just so refreshing and beautiful. The water was so pristine and unlike anything I had seen growing up in New Jersey. Don't get me wrong. I must digress. I am a true Jersey girl, and love this state. We have the best beaches and shore line. We have mountains; however small they may be, to ski, and we have a short distance to the greatest city in the world; New York. I need not say more. Getting back to the stream; we probably shouldn't have, but we drank from it. It was so refreshing. This place was truly a piece of Heaven on Earth.

We stayed there for quite a while as we waited for Dad to come down from the mountain, like the Israelites waited for Moses to come down from Mount Sinai. I could see the anxiety on my mother's face. It seemed like an eternity that we waited for him. I am sure my mother was thinking. "What If he doesn't come back? What if he crashes in that stupid Jeep? How am I going to raise these kids by myself?"

My father came back after some time, and like Moses, his face was radiant because he had experienced the beauty of the natural revelation of God through His creation on the top of that mountain peak. It was worth all of the aggravation to get there.

That was really a good trip.

I guess Dad was finally figuring out how to make a vacation great. This was probably the last trip that we took as a family. My sister had already gotten married and there was just the four of us. Soon, I would be graduating from high school, college, getting married, and living my life.

Now many years later, even after raising our three children, and welcoming four grandchildren into our family, I still treasure and laugh over our very unique kinds of family vacations. I appreciate the fact that even if my parents really didn't know how to "do" vacations, according to many people's standards, that they made the effort. More importantly, we were together. Now Mom has gone on to her place in Heaven, and Dad is in the Alzheimer's unit in a nursing home. He's not always cognizant, but as I prepared to write this story, I reminded him of our vacations and how we went to Utah. He started laughing, and said, "We never did find that lake. Did we Ruth?"

"No we didn't Dad."

I couldn't tell if that little smirk on his face was part of his dementia, or a moment of actual clarity. I would like to think it was the latter, but I got the feeling that he never really wanted to find that lake.

We laughed together for several moments. After all, what it comes down to, are memories of our experiences, places, and loved ones.

I am I grateful that our parents showed us many places in this beautiful, diverse, and vast country. There were visits to many other places, like Niagara Falls, Yellowstone, The Sequoia forest, that I didn't include in these memoirs.

As a child growing up, I almost saw it all, that is, except for Salt Lake, and the guy who jarred these memories, "The Old Man of the Mountain."

All the material goods we have accumulated mean nothing as our lives begin the descent into the unknown, uncharted places of disease, death, and finally into the glory of eternity. This becomes increasingly clear as I sit with my father day after day in this Alzheimer's unit. Now, living with Parkinson's, I wonder what my final days will look like. It haunts me beyond what I can even describe on paper. I will leave it at that.

Even with his flaws, just remembering Dad, the person he was, and the good times we shared, gives me a reason to remember and share these stories with whoever may come across these words that I have written down. Perhaps this chapter doesn't even fit with my journey with Parkinson's. Somehow I think it does. If I end up with no words, sitting in a care facility, seeing things that aren't really there, I hope people will realize that I once had a life, a mind, and that I was full of spirit, and I could laugh, cry, and feel joy and happiness.

Right now, without these memories, I would just feel sad. Dad's life wasn't in vain. He had three children, each who went on to have three children. Now these three children are having children. This family matters. Our place in the world has been sealed by God. Whatever state of existence that we end up in our later years, is only for a short season, and doesn't negate the lives that we have led. It is how you live your life and affect the people around you in a positive way while you still can. That is why I am writing. I hope I can encourage, and bring laughter and peace to those who are suffering.

$\mathcal{T}$hose Closest to Me

I feel I have left out a lot of information about how this disease has affected the members of my family. I would be negligent if I didn't mention the people that are dearest to me, the ones who love me the most, and who have been my greatest allies in fighting this insidious interruption to living a normal life, or at least what I think is a normal life.

To protect them, I really didn't want to discuss the details of how this disease has affected my children. There are some things that are too painful to disclose. Each one was a different age when they realized that there was something not quite right with Mom. Yet, I realize in order to tell the truth I should be honest about some of the changes and effects that my PD had on each child. All of them are adults now, and I have asked them for permission to tell our story.

Our oldest is our son, Stephen, whose love, concern and dedication to me has never wavered. He is extremely observant and thoughtful. He is in law enforcement and naturally he is always trying to help me and I know with his quiet but intuitive intelligence, he is always watching, and is there when he needs to be. His wife, Jessica, is in the medical profession and has been one of my greatest sources of encouragement, information and advice. She is the most wonderful daughter-in-law a woman can have. She always welcomes me into their home, and has allowed me to help take care of and play non-stop with their two beautiful children. Knowing what she knows about Parkinson's, I will be forever grateful to her to allow me to be so involved with those precious children My first grandson is now six and his sister is two.

My six year old grandson, Nicholas, like his dad, is extremely sensitive to my difficulties. The moment he sees me have a slight stumble in my step, he will give me that all knowing look, reach his hand back, and say, "Here, Nanu, I will show you how to walk." We continue on as we both march to some crazy imaginary beat, and somehow that tricks my brain into taking the next step.

My two year old granddaughter, Jillian just loves sitting on my lap, drinking her bottle and playing with my hair. Just recently, we were listening to the "Goat edition" of Tim McGraw singing "Truck Yeah" when my dyskinesia became unbearable, I could see her bouncing around, and I said, "Oh these movements!" She took her hand, put it on my leg, and said, "Moving, moving." She smiled at me and my heart melted for the millionth time. Whenever Jill sees me she comes running into my arms. That is worth all the dopamine in the world.

My second child, Elizabeth is a high school teacher. She is the quiet one about my disease. She just cries inside, and I know she wonders, "Why?"

My first memory of when I think Elizabeth noticed something was weird with her mom was when she and I spent a four day mother and daughter weekend at beautiful Camp Cherith, a Christian girl's camp, in upstate N.Y. We chose archery as our activity for the afternoon. As I was aiming for my target, my right foot was twisting so badly, that I literally dug a hole in the grass where I was standing. It is actually funny to me now. I just happened to see Elizabeth and her best friend, Amy with their hands over their mouths, looking like they were telling secrets. I heard Amy say, "What's wrong with your mother's foot?" I'm pretty sure they were cracking up, thinking it was amusing. I may be wrong. We never really discussed this. Elizabeth always gets a kick out of life and looks for the positive. She gets that from me. But I can remember the quirky looks on their faces and it must have made them laugh to see me aiming at a target with a bow and arrow, and digging a hole in the ground with my foot.

Camp Cherith is not an isolated example of me digging holes with my feet. It happens at soccer games, picnics, or at the beach. When I am outside, it happens all the time!

When we go to the beach, my feet move so much that there is usually a huge crater in front of my beach chair. I am forever filling in my holes! I know that anyone who sits with me, at the beach knows that this is going to happen. If I get up, and my chair is vacant, everyone knows that's my seat!

Elizabeth now has two little boys, and she too allows me to spend so much time with them. Her first son loves me to death. He gives his loves so freely. He is the active one, who challenges me physically! "You can do it," is his unspoken attitude. J.J. or John Jeffrey spoke very early. He said really big words before he even turned two. One time I "clicked off" at a family party. I was sitting there in my fog and J.J. said, "Nono, (his name for me), play with me."

I said, "I'm so sorry JJ. I can't walk right now."

"Nono drink water; take medicine!"

How precious and perceptive of him for being so incredibly observant at such a young age. It also bothered me that a child so young would grow to understand that his grandmother had a serious problem and was perhaps different from others. I love my grandkids so much. I want to be strong and be there for them. Maybe they are truly the ones that inspire me to fight harder.

I don't recommend this, but one time John caused me to realize that I may be capable of more than I think. His mom left me with J.J. (two and a half) and my newest grandson, Thomas (six months.) I was sitting there holding the baby, while almost completely clicked off, which meant I couldn't really walk. My daughter went out the front door to get in her car to get the pizza. The pizza place is just 1 minute away, so I figured it would be ok. Well the two year old ran out the front door after her. In my mind I thought, "Oh no, he could run behind the car. She wouldn't see him and she could hit him." I visualized this and in a split second I ran out the door holding the baby and grabbed him before he got to the driveway. Call it coincidence, timing of dopamine reaching the brain, adrenaline, or a combination of all these things. I don't really know. I call it a miracle. My life is full of miracles, that I find when I am just simply paying attention. I have heard other stories about how Parkinsonians have run out of burning houses.

Elizabeth's husband, Chris has a gentle, quiet, and thoughtful way of dealing with my Parkinson's. I can tell he is always thinking. Being a CPA, I'm sure he tries to analyze, and wonder how this thing can be fixed. He is very loving and has been faithfully walking by my side at the Unity Walk in Central Park, since I began my involvement about ten years ago. He is one of the faithful ones in joining my team and raising funds for this great cause. I know Chris will always be there for me. His sons look so much like him! He's going to be a great hockey coach to them.

Megan, my third child is perhaps the most difficult to talk about. The way that PD has affected my baby is profound. It has taken me a long time to even try to put it in perspective. She is the child who only knows me as a mom with Parkinson's disease.

I knew something wasn't right shortly after she was born. I have already gone into detail in previous parts of my memoirs, so I won't bore the reader with more details. By the time Megan was two years old, I was diagnosed, on meds, doing fairly well, and continuing on my journey, putting on my game face, and still trying to hide it. What I couldn't hide was my exhaustion. It is not easy being a mom to three children under the best of circumstances. Poor Megan, I would be coloring with her on her bedroom floor and sometimes I would fall asleep. She would have to wake me up.

As the years progressed, Megan became so attached to me. She had terrible separation anxiety, beyond what would be normal. She hated being away from me because she feared that something would happen to me.

I enrolled her in a Kinder-music class with a lovely sweet woman who directed it. The children were about three or four years old, and they learned to sing songs and play xylophones. As I left Megan there, it got progressively worse. She would cry the whole time, and finally she resorted to just lying on the floor in a fetal position sobbing until I returned. The director recommended that Megan leave the class. I totally agreed.

Several years later when she was in fourth grade, Megan's teacher suggested that she see the school counselor. At first I was a little taken back thinking, my daughter didn't need a counselor, but in hindsight, her short involvement with Megan brought out so many issues that Megan had developed directly relating to my Parkinson's. It took me by storm because I thought I had been doing a great job of hiding it from my children, especially her because she was so young, and had grown up with it. I know now, that some things cannot and should not be hidden. The fact is, I was secretly in denial, and that denial translated to Megan as "Why won't Mom be honest with me and tell me what's wrong with her?" We just didn't talk about these things. Maybe if I ignore it, it will go away, or no one will notice.

Although Megan did very well in school, and had lots of friends, she always hated going to school and still was worried about me while she was at school. This fear came to a full head in her sophomore year of high school, where she cried constantly, was extremely depressed, and happiness eluded her. There was no joy, only darkness day after day. We pulled her out of school. I spent the next few years homeschooling her which was rather daunting. She seemed to be doing better. We prayed feverishly for her. It would take several years for our prayers to be answered.

As Megan grew up she started coming into her own, and by her own strength and fortitude went to college in N.Y.C., and graduated with a Bachelor's Degree in Fashion Marketing and Merchandising. I can't tell you how proud we are of her.

When we were finally able to talk about my Parkinson's, Megan expressed her deep feelings and anger over the disease. She could not understand why I have it and why God would do this to me. She would say with anger in her voice and violently crying, "Mom, you are the best person. No one is better than you, and you don't deserve this."

Always trying to protect my children, I would respond with "I'm fine. I'm OK Meg."

Now, screaming back at me, "No you're not fine, Mom. Why don't you admit it, you're not Ok!"

I would insist that I was fine. To have said, "I am not fine," would have been like defeat for me. Denial still reared its ugly head.

Megan needed to hear that it was ok to be angry. It wasn't ok that she had to deal with this disease and worry about me all the time. She needed to know that she had no control over it and had to accept the fact that her mom was fighting a degenerative brain disease. She was too young to understand all of this. I have to be so honest here and finally admit that it was my Parkinson's and her knowledge of it that has made life so hard for Megan.

This is for you, Meg, I know that now. You are so right. It isn't fair. It sucks! I really don't understand it. I remember that painful Christmas when you came into my room late at night sobbing and told me face to face how you really felt. I listened, but almost didn't want to hear it. I just wanted everyone to be all right, especially you that night. I know nothing I said really eased your pain. Hopefully, our long tearful mother and daughter embrace was enough for that night. I am sorry that I never realized it until I wrote these memoirs. It was Christmas night, and I was tired. In hindsight, I wish I could have done more for you, but it seemed like nothing I said made sense to you. This still pains me. That being said, I hope you can still have faith in God and His plans for you, me, and the future.

Megan recently celebrated her twenty-ninth birthday. She is in the fashion Industry, and is also a certified Yoga Instructor. I have learned so much from this child, who has always been beautiful; inside and out. She has brought me to my knees in prayer. She has taught me to be honest with myself, and others, to be patient, to ask for help when I need it…..to just talk and not bottle things up.

She can also be pretty hard on me, which sometimes I need. Exercise, yoga, eat right, and wait until my meds kick in before I lunge forward and crash into a table or go down on all fours. She wants me to go places with her. She's willing to put up with me. "Oh come on Mom. You can do it. Just march…. one, two, three, four." Somehow this gets the brain in gear.

I wrote a lot about Megan because she is the child that clearly struggled with my disease the most. I know my other two children love me just as much, as I do them. They had a "normal" mom, when they were younger. There are six years between Elizabeth and Megan and nine years between Megan and Stephen. Maybe she was so attached to me because I didn't let go of her, afraid of what this disease was going to eventually do to me. I still struggle with that. Perhaps I over-indulged her because I somehow felt guilty, as if I could even control the progression of the disease. Who really knows? God will explain it to me someday when I see Him face to face.

I have been saving the last person to write about. That is my husband, Jeffrey. I don't even really know where to begin. A lot of what we have shared together is so personal and private. He is not really a "Let me express my feelings" kind of guy. I say that, yet Jeff is the one whose eyes well up with tears singing praise music in church, or watching a tear jerker movie or television show about family, kids, or pets. For the most part, he keeps his concerns about me on the inside. Even though he worries about me, at the same time, he treats me no differently. I like that. If I need sympathy, he is the guy to give it to me. If I want to pretend I'm normal and fly by the seat of my pants heaped up on Carbidopa-Levodopa, he goes with that, too. He puts up with my quilting and sewing obsession at 5:00 am, and he waits for me to "click on" before going anywhere. That requires a lot of patience, something he has had to learn over the years. He is sympathetic, and kind. The thing that I love most about Jeff is that he loves me so much. Our love has grown into a beautiful thing over the last forty-one years of marriage. He still finds me beautiful and says he is so blessed to have me for his wife. That really amazes me, dyskinesia and all. I am not sure that I would be that enthralled with a spouse moving all over the place kicking me under the table, or on the other hand, so clicked off that I can't walk. He is truly an amazing man. I love him with all my heart.

Lately I feel that I have come to appreciate him so much more. We share such a great friendship. We were practically children when we met. I was seventeen and he was eighteen. It was my first year of college.

I went to a fairly conservative Christian College in Massachusetts. I had been spreading my wild oats so to speak, the summer before college, and managed to still spread a few, that year, as I dodged the people who could have gotten me in trouble in my dorm….normal stuff for a seventeen year old girl from New Jersey in the 1970s. I will leave it at that.

I had started thinking that I really didn't fit in at this school, and was in the process of making plans to transfer to another school, perhaps with a more partying agenda. My wise parents just waited this out. But I was pretty miserable. I loved my classes, and most of my professors, but I just wasn't having any fun. This was a reason to transfer, right?

Anyway, that all changed after December of 1971. One of my friends brought Jeff back to the dorm lobby with one of his friends. At this time men were not allowed to visit in our dorm rooms. My friend came running up to my room announcing that she had two "Really cute guys" in the lobby. There was this bloodhound dog, named "Dinky," (A popular dog name back then) that used to roam around our dorm. I quickly configured a plan to see these guys without them noticing me by pretending to chase "Dinky" through the lobby, and nonchalantly take a quick peek at the young men. I did just that. Years later, in remembering this, Jeff said that he wondered what the heck this girl was doing chasing after some goofy dog in the lobby. At least he looked, too.

At first I wasn't impressed with him, and evidently he wasn't too impressed with me. In fact, I told my friend that I thought the other guy was cute. So, I think she was going to set her sights on Jeff. To tell you the truth, I didn't even give it another thought.

Something had stirred, and someone else had given it a thought; a thought that was whispered a jillion years before the beginning of time, called "destiny," or as I like to put it, God.

Several nights later, Jeff called me. His grandmother had just died, and he just felt he needed someone to talk to. It is the strangest thing, how he would call me right out of the blue, when something so sadly personal had happened in his world, and we barely even knew each other. I told him to come over. He did.

We went for a ride; a very long ride. He drove to the beach, which happens to be my favorite place. I will never forget that night as long as I live. It wasn't even a date, but we bonded in a way, that two humans who just met, very rarely bond. I will be up front. It wasn't physical, but spiritual, and emotional. We spoke about our deepest feelings. After that ride, my life would never be the same. I knew that I wanted this boy, with every fiber of my mind and body. I felt such passion.

Our first real date was to an Emmerson, Lake, and Palmer concert. You have to be a child born in the '50s or '60s to know who they were, I believe. That was when the "Moog" synthesizer was the coolest thing in rock music. It all started with "Switched on Bach." This was the beginning of electronic music. Now when we are going through our I-tunes, on one of our Saturday nights down the shore with my brother and his wife, we play these oldies, and laugh hysterically, but it's still cool. By the way, their most famous song is titled, "Lucky Man."

To make a very long, happy, and sometimes sad story of life, shorter than it really deserves to be, Jeff and I will be celebrating our forty-second wedding anniversary this coming April. We are an example of a couple who has weathered the highs and lows of marriage, the raising of three exceptional children, saying good bye to some of our dearest loved ones, and presently battling a debilitating brain disease. It's funny, but as I think back, the picture of our lives together could have been perfect, without Parkinson's, but it really wasn't. We had a great marriage, but it wasn't void of stupid arguments, hurting each other's feelings, and treating each other with less than what we deserved. Sometimes we were selfish. What it amounts to is nonsense, triviality, and lack of communication. We always loved each other, and put God first in our marriage. That was the glue that held us together.

After my diagnosis, and going through many storms together, we have come to realize what is really important. That is why I get so upset with couples these days, who fight over things that do not matter; little things. The saying, "Youth is wasted on the young," is so true. I never really understood it until I got older. Wisdom really does come with age. You realize what works, what is important, and what really isn't worth wasting your time on. You learn to take a deep breath and then continue.

We were young and stupid once, too. Jeff and I had a full blown fight over a hot dog our first year of marriage. We were eating hot dogs in the little shack that we called home back then, a one bedroom cottage attached to a large farmhouse. It was tiny, and our pipes froze in the winter. Getting back to the fight.... As I remember it, I didn't want to eat my second hot dog, and so I left it. Jeff thought I was being wasteful. His parents used to make him eat everything on his plate. Mine didn't. This sounds so stupid but I got really mad and threw the hot dog at him. I had never done this before, and I almost felt a surge of violence…scary stuff. Well, it got even scarier. He went and got a pillow and threw it at me! The memory of this creates a really funny image in my mind; however, at the time I really thought that I was experiencing some sort of domestic violence. It really was upsetting, even though it was the most stupid argument there ever was. How ridiculous. We never threw anything at each other again.

Incidentally, that little cottage and the farmhouse burned down one December night that brought with it, lightening, snow, and severely cold weather. We were acutely aware of this because our pipes had frozen again. We didn't know what caused the fire. It could have been that the landlord had been up in the attic with a blow torch trying to thaw our pipes, lightning striking, or bad wiring setting on fire. We will never know. The miracle was that a family with seven children lived in the farm house, and the little dog started barking, woke up the family, and all nine people were unhurt and ran out of that house. The next thing Jeff and I were aware of as we lay sleeping, huddled together in the cold night, we heard screaming and glass breaking, "Jeff, Ruth get out, **Fire!**"

We were left unscathed physically, but not emotionally by this ghastly fire. The fire quickly engulfed the farmhouse, but its path stopped right where our cottage was joined to it. We lost nothing. Even our cat, Flower, and her kitten, Spotty, made it out safely. I think this was the first time I really realized a miracle had occurred in our lives. The family, however, lost all of their belongings. The family was poor, but luckily they did have insurance and were able to build a nice new home very quickly. My parents loaned us about $3,000.00, for a down payment on a house, and we bought our first house and moved in within two weeks. You would never see that happening now-a-days, not the small down payment nor the quick mortgage and moving into a house in just two weeks! You might say that this experience changed us dramatically. We were no longer kids, but we were adults, and now we held on to each other for dear life. We were officially glued together as a family who had just lived through our first real storm. I can remember it as if it were yesterday, not fifteen thousand, three hundred thirty-three yesterday's ago, if I did the math right.

Our marriage was filled with normal ups and downs. We have always been faithful to each other, because we really love each other, and in our heads we are still those crazy teenagers who are wild about each other. Why would we stray when we have the best of the best right here in front of us?

A disease may tend to break families up, at times. In our case, because of who we are, it made us stronger. I think it is because Jeff is the man that he is. I want to get it into writing that I don't know what I would do without him. He is a tower of strength to me. I think I have been a wife that he has been able to run to after the battle each day of trying to provide for his family, and make a living, which has involved long commutes into the city on a daily basis. He also managed to get his college degrees at night school after more years than I'd like to remember. Now those years are pretty much a blur. Two of our children actually went to his commencement.

What an example of perseverance Jeff has been. Little did he know his ability to persevere would really be an ally to him as he continues to love me in spite of myself or what this disease is doing and will do to me. I just hope God doesn't need him sooner than He needs me.

Jeff has also been a great father to his children. He always had time for them. Now he is "Pop Pop" and his grandchildren will attest that they love him so much. When Pop-Pop is around, Nanu is put on second string. Everyone wants to sit next to him. Sometimes I get a little jealous. Other times, I am glad for the break.

Have I mentioned that Jeff is also an incredibly beautiful man? His eyes are a lovely shade of hazel, and they are the kindest eyes you have ever seen. He gets that from his mom.

In his youth, he was the strongest man on the earth. I really mean that. He single handily moved our piano up a flight of about five stairs from our family room to our living room. Not to mention a few other "Super Hero" acts such as lifting an engine block, having the landing gear of an airplane fall on his head, and another time his hair getting caught in a drill press. He was an aircraft mechanic for several years when we were first married. He never has been one to ask for outside help from others. Now however, probably as a result of all the aforementioned activities, getting older has robbed Jeff of a lot of strength because of bad knees, family history, arthritis, and Type II Diabetes. If you ask me, though, he is still the greatest super hero and strongest man around.

The rest of my family has stood beside me for the last twenty-five or so years. However, we suffered much loss in 2015. As I write now, my tears start to fall for the first time since I started my so called "Book" or "Memoirs." I was by my mother's side as she took her last painful breath, and watched the artery in her neck stop pulsing and she went to be with Jesus. I will never forget the look of death that came upon her. I know my son tried to get me out of the room before she died, but I needed to be there. I then knew her suffering was over and after a lifetime of watching and praying over me and all her children, grandchildren, great grandchildren, and living a life of service to others, she was dancing with Jesus. However, the pain of missing her will never go away until I see her again.

The thing about this particular day that struck me as another way God's hand is in every moment of our lives, is that my niece, Tara, Bill and Linda's daughter gave birth to a beautiful baby girl. The fact that the baby was perfect was a miracle in itself as Tara has battled chronic Lyme disease for several years. Jason, Tara's husband was by her side. They named the baby Brooklyn Grace. My mom's name was Grace. After wondering why God had waited so long to take my mom, and challenging my faith, because I couldn't understand why she had to suffer so much, the birth of this child, answered all my questions. He had to complete one life and bring forth another. This may seem like nonsense to some. I just know how it made me feel and how it strengthened my faith. It made so much sense to me. Sometimes God's ways seem mysterious to us, but our questions will all be answered, some day.

As I mentioned before, after a life of hard work and perseverance as an electrical engineer, business owner, World War II veteran, my dad is ninety-three years old and still struggling along in the Alzheimer's unit of a care facility. This is a painful reminder of how unfair life can be.

After my mother passed away, I wasn't sure that I would be able to go to the care facility where my father lives. It's not always easy because he is so confused between reality and the fantasy life of jumbled up memories in his head. He tells me that I am the only one that matters. He loves me so much that it is almost suffocating. He wants to kiss and hold my hand the whole time. I truly think that he thinks I am my mother. Recently, he referred to her as "The other one who died."

I said, "You mean Mom?"

He said, "Yeah, the other wife." Wow! On one hand it really bothers me, and on the other it's ok because it's not his fault. The confusion just consumes him. I try to just go along with it. But when it comes to me being his wife, I set him straight, "I am Ruth Anne your daughter. I have a husband, children, and grandchildren." He just looks at me with one of those "whatever," looks.

During a very recent visit Dad did the funniest thing. I laugh when I think about it. My brother and I happened to visit at the same time. We were talking to each other when out of the corner of my eye I saw Dad dialing his hand as if it were a phone, an old fashioned dial phone. After he dialed a few times, he brought the phone, his cupped hand, to his ear and said, "Hi Joe, I'll pick you up in twenty minutes. I am polishing my sword right now."

Bill and I just looked at each other. I have to laugh and think it's funny or it will drive me crazy.

We lost our precious dog Roxy, at the beginning of 2016. I still cry for her because she loved me so much. She was always by my side, and kept walking with me, until her hips gave out and she could no longer breathe. She wasn't trained to be a service dog, but she was. You may wonder why we haven't gotten another dog. After all, that is the only thing that heals the pain of the loss of a beloved dog. I think at this point, I am still able to travel, and after all, a dog is a lot of work. As my husband and I get older, we think it's best to move past wanting another dog. We can babysit for our son's crazy dog when we get the urge. That usually cures us. We do have a cat named Willie that Megan brought home. He is a nut and drives me nuts. He causes so much trouble, but now he is always by my side.

For my brother and sister, I have nothing but love. My brother is one of my heroes. He is always there for me and he still makes me laugh uncontrollably. His wife is amazing, and I love her as a true sister. She had to pick me up at 7:00 in the morning, as I sat on the sidewalk down the shore because I couldn't walk. I thought I was fine and was "clicked-on" when I decided to walk to the bakery and get our favorite crumb buns. I could feel the "FOG" setting in, and tried to make it home, but ended up on the sidewalk with my crumb buns next to me. It was early in the morning. Many people jogged and rode bikes past me. I couldn't believe that no one even stopped to ask me if I was ok. But, Linda pulled up in her car and helped me in. She never once was horrified at her grown sister-in-law in a heap on the sidewalk, but she just casually started talking, brought me home, sat with me, had coffee, and crumb buns. No big deal. I will always be grateful for her love and support. She makes me feel normal. That is a great thing.

I know it pains my sister to see me sometimes. She feels so deeply, like Megan. She is very private, and doesn't understand what is happening to me. My disease overwhelms her and I totally understand. It is hard to understand. She wonders how I can do what I do with the terrible dyskinesia. I just do it as best as I can. It upsets her though and that is sad for me.

My nieces and nephews and their spouses, and children are all wonderful as well. They love me and I believe they always see me and not the disease. Some have their own health issues and we can commiserate together.

An example of their love and dedication to me recently became so real to me. My husband and I had an extended weekend vacation in Charleston, South Carolina with my brother and his entire family. We had a great time walking the beautiful famous streets of Charleston with names like King, Queen, Market St. Meeting, and Bay St. Charleston is such a charming city, and walking them is irresistible. We walked everywhere, which was quite a feat for me. I couldn't believe how much I walked that weekend. However, one evening after eating a delicious meal at one of Charleston's famous eateries, I think I ate too much protein. I'm not sure that I ever mentioned the fact that Parkinson's medication is very easily absorbed by protein and then "clicking on" becomes virtually impossible for a long time, maybe even hours.

We ate this wonderful meal, and I probably had a glass or two of wine. We had about a mile to walk, at night. When my husband and I said good night to everyone, I was still ok. They were going to continue the party at another location. We decided to call it a wrap a little earlier. After walking all day, and still not done my hips, legs, etc., were killing me. Jeff's knees and back were also killing him. Getting old is so much fun, even naturally getting old.

We started our journey back to the hotel. Jeff wanted to stop at Walgreen's to get some water. I literally, stumbled into the store, very "clicked-off." I managed to make my way to some stools by Walgreen's front window. I must have looked so forlorn, and pathetic, as I wondered how the heck I was going to make it back to the hotel. Being my stubborn self, I would have no talk about getting an Uber car.

As I sat there, I heard banging on the window. At first it made me jump, but when I looked again, it was my nephews, Bill, his wife Lauren, and Scott, and his girlfriend.

They came in. It didn't take them long to realize my condition. When Jeff was done shopping, the four of those faithful angels watched over us and walked us slowly and carefully right to the door of our hotel. I will never forget this as long as I live. It was like a procession, with me slowly leading the way. The beat of Lauren's boots hitting the sidewalk, kept me focused on putting one foot in front of the other.

I hope to be an inspiration to them, pray for them, and just be there for all of them, as well.

Creativity and Parkinson's

PLWPS develop a very intimate relationship with their brains. We think about them all the time. I speak for myself, but it must be true for the entire Parkinson's community. Every minute we are aware of the chemicals, or lack of them flowing through our nervous system. It is a daunting statement to say that Parkinson's is a disorder of the central nervous system. That sounds like a really important neurological and physiological system, doesn't it? Therefore, if I manage to get the right amount of L-Dopa flowing to my brain, I sometimes forget to take my meds. Just to remind the reader, L-Dopa is an amino acid and is converted into dopamine and is used to treat Parkinson's. By the way, dopamine is a monoamine neuro transmitter that is essential for nerve activity. As I was saying, I forget for a very brief time. This is a problem. It puts me at risk for all my full blown symptoms to very quickly re-surface. I go through this on a daily basis, as mentioned before. Not always because I forget to take meds, but because it is so hard to get the precise amount of dopamine to the brain at the precise time. That is why they have created controlled release medications. They don't really work that great for me. But that's just me.

As part of this awareness of my brain, I am aware of certain changes in my cognitive life, so to speak. One of those changes that can occur, due to a certain medication, is that people may exhibit compulsions, in one or more areas. This may not be a bad thing, in fact it can be one of the positive aspects of Parkinson's, if there is any.

However, when the brain chemistry causes negative compulsive behavior it can be extremely serious and threaten a person's livelihood, and even cost them their families. One side effect is the compulsion to gamble. My doctor told me that she has had patients succumb to this temptation and she had to immediately pull them off this particular medication, even though it is a very helpful aid in treating symptoms. Other compulsions reported are having extra marital affairs, and sexual obsessions. Thankfully, I don't have any of these.

My obsession is sewing! To be specific: making purses, of all things. It all started early one morning while I was getting ready for work. Megan called me into her room and said, "Mom I'm opening up an on-line Etsy Shop. I'm calling it Megan and Elizabeth, and you're going to make purses!"

My response was "Are you crazy, I don't know how to make purses. What are you talking about?"

Megan doesn't sew, but has a great sense of fashion and style. She is also great at giving other people ideas, for example, me. She has always had this power over me, and can talk me into almost anything. It's fascinating as well as maddening. I say this with humor and love. I have often told her that she should have been a lawyer, because she is so convincing. But really, making pocketbooks is the last thing I wanted to do. It's not like I didn't have anything to do and needed another hobby. I work, I babysit, I cook, clean, and battle a brain disease, every minute of the day and night. What was she talking about?!

Soon after, she gave me a Martha Stewart video of a lady making clutches. For some reason, it looked easy, and like great fun. Wow, maybe we could make money doing this…..It didn't take long for me to try to make clutches. They started out pretty weird and lop-sided, but I'm a fast learner, and after many failures, they started coming together. I started making purses, lots of purses. I couldn't stop. I became so excited about fabric. I began buying fabric on line. Early in the morning I would pour through fabric web sites and just marvel over all the gorgeous fabrics available. Ordering fabric became my obsession. I would impatiently and excitedly wait for it to arrive, and then I would sew. I graduated from making small clutches, to full-size envelope purses, tote bags, overnight duffel bags, change purses, laptop carrier totes, beach bags, diaper bags, and our most popular request, yoga mat bags.

At one point Megan saw my obsession, and said, "Mom, Stop! You're obsessed."

My only response, in self-defense was, "Well, you made me this way, when you told me I was going to make purses. I listened to you."

We have had the on-line shop for several years now. We have sold a lot of items. My best customer is my sister-in-law, Linda. I have made many custom bags for her, and she swears off all other brands. She is still, my faithful supporter.

I can't say that I can quit my day job, nor would I want to, but I love making bags!! One of my neurologists calls me, "The Bag Lady." Every time I see him he asks, "Are you still making purses?" to which I respond, "Oh yes, here and there." He says as long as I'm not awake all night obsessed with making purses; it's a very positive side effect of the meds. But they make sure they ask me every visit. I always act nonchalant, but secretly I can still be obsessed. I love it. It gives me a creative release, and I think it's great for the brain. Math is involved in measuring, and the creativity in putting together the bags, and coming up with new ideas has to be good for my brain. The fabrics and colors bring me such joy.

Since I've been doing this, I have realized how perfectly accurate my measurements must be. The problem is that I've never been a perfectionist. I am definitely a "Jack of all trades; master of none." But I have become much more accurate, and if something doesn't look right, I take it apart and re-do it. After all, I am selling the item to someone, and it should be perfect. People use their hard earned money to buy our products. Friends and family say we should go on that show, "The Shark Tank". I laugh and say, "They would eat us up alive, when they ask how much we have sold, and what are our profits?" We also have way too much inventory, because of my obsession. Ha! I am doing this for the love of it, and perhaps Megan does it for me and hangs in there as the CEO. I have to laugh because she is supposedly the boss. However, I buy the fabric (on the company's credit card). I design, make, and ship all the bags and then communicate to the customer the shipping date.

That being said, Megan is still one of my main muses. She inspires me, makes me a better person, and makes me work with integrity. She is extremely good at quality control, and lets me know when I need to fix something. I try to get away with it, but she always calls me out. I know she is usually right even when I try to explain things away. It doesn't work. She really is good at what she does. I'm getting there, too!

Keep in mind that sewing and using a foot pedal to make the machine sew, is quite difficult when your foot is twisting and turning and you're trying to sew a straight line, when your body is going every which way. I end up with such cramps in my legs, feet, and arms. I grit my teeth and clench my jaw, but I'll be darned if Parkinson's is going to take away something I love to do so much. I must be a glutton for punishment. It's a wonder I have never run over my fingers with the machine's sewing needle.

After my mom passed away, we cleaned out her house. We found piles and piles of fabric, hidden everywhere. It was in every closet, under every bed, and stashed away in the basement and even the garage. Needless to say, I took all of it home and now it is stashed up in my attic.

Mom was a master quilter, and made dozens of beautiful, hand sewn heirloom quilts. Her stitches were all done by hand and were impeccable. She never sold a quilt, unlike her daughter, who would sell anything! She put all her heart and soul into her quilts.

My mom taught me to sew when I was a little girl. I spent the entire summer before high school, making my own clothes. It was so much fun. So I really have enjoyed sewing in the past.

In addition to the purses, I also make quilts now as my obsession with fabric, and putting things together continues. I love starting a new quilt. My favorite part is in the planning of the quilt and cutting out all of the little pieces. I wake up early, and sit on the floor in the middle of my sewing room, and cut out little squares of fabric. I lay them on the bed, and experiment with placing the colors in the right order. Every color and every square is thought about. I am the creator, and I want the finished product to be my masterpiece. That is what God thinks about when He creates His children, His masterpieces. He puts all the right combinations together to form what to Him is what he wants us to be.

The quilt that I am finishing up right now is a type of color wheel design. It is my favorite, so far. I started out where the middle of the quilt will be, piecing 2.5 inch squares together. I began with very pale colored squares. I placed them in rows in a sort of pixilated presentation. I labored over the placing of every square of fabric. Nothing was placed in a random manner. The muted colors eventually led the way to brighter colors, and now the quilt's edges are very bright, darker, and distinct. They are much sharper. When I was finished piecing hundreds of little squares together, I hand quilted circles starting in the middle and circling out to the edges. This is where I am at right now. The first circle is very small, maybe a two -inch diameter. From there I sewed circles that have about a half an inch between them. They become very large as I work my way out from the center to the edges. The circles give a beautiful continuity to the quilt. They make the colors melt into each other and form their connection to each other as one unified display of color. When the quilt is finished, it will become a beautiful mosaic of color and have a life of its own.

Like my mother, I realized after making this quilt that I could never sell it. It's like a baby to me, my creation; just like I am to God, His creation. I wouldn't change a thing about my quilt. I lovingly placed every square of it together. Even with all its flaws, it is perfect to me. God has placed all my pieces together onto His blueprint or pattern of my life, my journey. To God I am perfect, because He made me that way.

> *"You created my inmost being; you knit me together in my mother's womb. I praise you because I am fearfully and wonderfully made; your works are wonderful, I know that full well." Psalm 139:14 and 15*

What I am trying to say is that I am by no means perfect, not even close. What I would like to be is a reflection of God who is perfect. Forget about me. I am nothing. Parkinson's makes me feel like less than nothing as I have expressed before. The only good in me comes from God. I wait for Him to pour out His blessings on me all the time, and I remain forever open to them. I'm not talking about material things, but about people, my family, relationships, memories, places, and events that matter. Everything else is just rubble and will be thrown away, sold, or destroyed. There is so much more to life than possessions. It is hard to keep that in mind when all day and night images of greed and self –gratification are thrown into our paths of vision. I guess a debilitating brain disease really brings out what is truly important to a person. It's really too bad that most people cannot realize this until something devastating comes into their lives.

I can't help making an analogy between my quilt and to my experience as a Parkinsonian. At the start of my journey my future seemed pale, muted, and unclear. It was just like the middle of the quilt. I couldn't see a glimpse of what the big picture was going to be. As the patchwork quilt of my life continues to be pieced together by my Creator, I have begun to see things a bit clearer. My destiny is unfolding as He molds me into the person He wants me to be; a person that will glorify God and not man. Whether, the quilt of my life becomes ripped, wrinkled, and of no earthly good, the greater purpose will be to have God use me in helping others to see Him, and reach my final destination, eternity with Jesus, my mom, and all the loved ones that have gone before me into His presence. I know the physical end of life is not pretty for any of us, but for those who love Jesus, and made Him master of our lives, there is joy beyond death. This is what keeps me going.

> *"Now we see but a dim reflection as a mirror, then we shall see face to face. Now I know in part, but then I will know fully, even as I am fully known." I Corinthians 13:12*

> *"All the days ordained for me were written in your book before one of them came to be." Psalm 139: 16*

Whether we like the finished product that we have become is of no consequence, but what we do with what we have been given is of great consequence, for both now and eternity. I believe in destiny, and so I hope that I am beautiful to God, and am exactly what He wants me to be... pathetic as I feel at times. I just hope others see Him in me.

> *"Yet you, Lord are our Father. We are the clay, you are the potter; we are all the work of your hand." Isaiah 64:8*

November 28, 2016

I got up early this morning; early being 3:15 a.m. Why did I get up so early? I got up early because I have Parkinson's disease. My brain bounces around because of the side effects of its levels of dopamine. Not only is my brain bouncing, but my body as well. I am being racked by severe dyskinesia. I get up partly because I don't want to wake Jeff up. He is tired too and deserves to sleep.

As I sit at the computer to type my thoughts, it is difficult to type. If I didn't correct my mistakes, my words would be unreadable because my fingers are hitting all the wrong keys. I should try to type a sample of what my uncorrected typing would be. I will type: "My name is Ruth Anne Drown. I have been a Parkinsonian for approximately twenty-seven years. I cannot remember what it feels like, to be a person living without Parkinson's." Ok, here we go.

My namre is Rthanne d
Rowon I have been oiving with ap rkinso s roe aproximtatlyk 27 uear
s. Icann9t remember withat it feels like to be a person living without
Parkinson;s

Wow! It was worse than I thought. In order for me to type correctly I have to concentrate really hard and try to squeeze my legs together as they flail all over the place. I kick the computer desk by accident. I inadvertently hit the wrong keys on the keyboard. I had to stop for several moments to remember the word, "keyboard". I have to laugh. I don't really know if that was because I have PD or just because I'm getting older. As I type, I just make corrections. It takes longer than it should. However, frustrating this must sound to a normal person, to me I am happy today, because I can still type!

As my self-described "roller coaster" day continues, it is now 5:11 am and the effects of the ½ a pill I took an hour ago are starting to wear off. I start to feel really good. I can type smoothly with relatively fewer mistakes. I am typing much slower now. It feels good, but I know what is coming…. If I don't take another ½ a pill, I won't be able to type, walk, or even think clearly. My mind will become shrouded with the darkness that Parkinson's places like a veil in front of my eyes. I can't imagine what a normal person would think about this. I would wonder, "How can a person deal with such contrasting existences, one, of extreme energy, bouncing all over the place, and the other, that resorts to lying on the couch, motionless, and can barely even communicate." Before I write another word, I have to take a pill. Oh no, I stopped to make a few corrections, and have probably missed my golden opportunity of making the transition of "off" to "on" smoother.

I am back now; not completely "on," but I will try my best. I have been awake for 2.5 hours. I put away my dishes from last night. After all yesterday was Thanksgiving. I did a lot. I should have been able to sleep. Yesterday, I also got up at 3:00 am. I put the turkey in the oven and finished preparing the rest of the food. In the past few days, I made sweet potatoes, squash, two kinds of stuffing, mashed potatoes, an apple pie, a blueberry pie, (all from scratch), and who knows what else. I cleaned the house, and rearranged some furniture so we'd have more room. I hoisted myself up to the attic to bring down some extra chairs.

Thanksgiving dinner was ready by 12:30 pm. The kids were all here. We had a great time, until the babies all needed naps and they cleared out by about 5:00 pm. It was a wonderful time for me. I mostly played with the grandkids, once the dinner was on the table.

After such busy days, you would think I would be able to sleep. Well now I am totally clicking off. My legs are shaking, and I am going to have to lie down until the meds click on again. So, I will save my addition to my story, and see what happens….maybe I will actually sleep for a few moments.

I am back after sleeping for about five minutes. While I was lying on the couch, I kept looking at the computer screen and my mind started racing, thinking of things I want to write about. I hopped over to the computer and wanted to write about things. Now I sit here in a fog, unable to remember everything. So sad…I thought my meds were clicking in. Another nasty reminder of what my doctor warns me about. It is not good for my brain to have so much Carbidopa/ Levodopa, or however you spell it. I will check it later. The drastic changes in chemical levels are probably not good, but what am I supposed to do? I beg the scientists. "Please find some way of helping us cope better with Parkinson's. If there are robots that will someday have emotions and people fear will take over the world, why can't science fix me?" I guess I will have to leave that up to God….back to the couch to try to sleep.

It is now 6:05 am. I was feeling pretty depressed lying there when all of a sudden my feet starting wiggling, and my meds are now clicking in. Now I am typing really fast again. My feet are tapping up and down, and my brain is firing on all levels. I will try not to sound to manic, although that is exactly how I feel. Now I am "positive Ruth." I feel good and I can express myself clearer.

While I was lying on the couch trying to sleep I saw a photo of my mom and me flash on the computer screen. We have that thing where all our photos do a slide show when the computer is in a certain mode. Anyway, in the photo, I looked between three and four years old and my mom was pregnant with my brother. My mom had put a few curlers in my hair. I looked so happy. I know I was by the smile on my face. I loved my mom so much. She was everything to me, my whole world. As a child I never wanted to be away from her. If she left me with a neighbor, I would pretty much cry the whole time. She rarely left me, except for if she had to go for a doctor's appointment or something.

I have to interrupt myself right here to add that I had to go back to the couch because I had a false alarm. I felt my meds working, I started to write again, and then I started shaking and freezing again. So I lay down, rested for a few, and then really started to "click on." I needed to communicate that, because I don't want to lose my focus on the fact that this is a journey with Parkinson's and that is what it does to me. I remind myself that my mission was to write for others who are suffering, with a diagnosis of PD. or for anyone that struggles with disease in any shape or form, so that they know that they are not alone. I feel as if I am giving a voice to the changes that happen, both physically and mentally.

I digress back to Mom. As I was mentioning, I had separation anxiety as a child from my mom because I loved her so much. I see so many similarities comparing my separation anxiety to Megan's. I think I just realized that.

When I was in kindergarten, I had a really mean old teacher. She should have retired years before I ever entered her classroom. I cried so hard to go home because I missed my mom. Why would I be happy with this old hag who just yelled at me for crying? I was afraid of her. One time we were sitting in a circle doing hand movement things to little poems like, "Here's the church, here's the steeple. Open the church; where's all the people? Here's the church; here's the steeple. Open the church; there are all the people." This was really challenging stuff. If you were born in the 50's, you know exactly what I am talking about. When we left the circle and lined up to go outside, the teacher noticed a large wet puddle on the floor. She hollered and screamed: "Who wet their pants. Which one of you did it?" We all stood there in line looking at each other. I remember thinking. "Oh no, did I wet my pants?" I didn't think I did, but you never know. I wet the bed sometimes at four years old. Well, no one confessed. She kept the inquisition going; still, no confession. I want to type the name of a female dog, but I just can't. Anyway, she went up that line and stuck her hand under every skirt, and every crotch of all of us in line until she came to the guilty party. I remember to this day, who he was. Poor little guy. I was so thankful it wasn't me. I don't remember what happened next. I just know that it was traumatic for me. I would never humiliate a child that way, or even worse, a whole class of children. In my career of teaching hundreds of children at the elementary level, or teaching piano, or Sunday school, I would never dream of subjecting children to this level of degradation. No wonder I missed my mom.

Mom has been gone now for almost two years. I still miss her. Sometimes I want to talk to her so badly. I just have things I want to tell her or questions I have about sewing or cooking. If I get exciting news, like a new grandchild is born, or Megan is going out with a really great guy now, I want to share it with her. Sometimes it's gossipy stuff. God forgive me. "Have you heard about this or that?" We used to talk almost every day. If I had a problem, she would help me figure out how to solve it. I didn't need a therapist because I had Mom. I probably should have a therapist! In fact, I know I should. Everyone could use one at some point in their lives.

Sometimes I will be driving to work, and I just cry out, "Can you see me Mom? I miss you. I want to talk to you! Can you please give me some sort of a sign?" I drive and I look all around for some kind of a sign from her. Is this ridiculous? Then somehow the Lord brings me comfort. I think she can see me. On a few occasions since her death, I have felt signs when

I was least expecting them. I don't know if it was really her or God helping me cope with my loss, by sending me a real spiritual dosage of the peace of her presence, sometimes in real physical things, or an inner voice speaking to me, not in a psychotic way, if you are thinking that!

The days following her burial, I was looking for signs. I go back to a conversation I had with Mom once. We were so close that I felt that when she died she would somehow communicate with me, that everything I have spent my whole life believing was true. That asking Jesus into my heart as a child, believing in every word of the Bible as the infallible word of God, that Christmas and Easter are all true, that Heaven really does exist, marrying a Christian man, attending church, raising our children in a Christian home, and that right now she is in God's presence, and I should never be afraid that it isn't true. I can't believe that I actually wrote all that, but this is truly how I felt those days almost two years ago. I don't at all believe that you can communicate with people who have gone on, but I did have that conversation. It was sort of tongue in cheek. But after she died, I was just hoping for something special from the Lord.

I can honestly point to three specific incidents. Objectively they might mean nothing to someone, but to me they were very real and spoke to my need in a powerful way.

The first sign, so to speak, happened two days after her burial. We walked into church and the theme was **"GRACE WINS."** All the volunteers, who basically keep our church running smoothly, were wearing tee shirts that said, **"GRACE WINS"**, my mom's name. Jeff and I just looked at each other when we walked in. I was overwhelmed. The theme of all the songs we sang was **"Grace"** There were banners with **"Grace"** written on them. I know the theme that Sunday was God's grace. But to me it was God giving me a sign that I so desperately needed. How could have I ever doubted Him? I was filled with the knowledge that it is all true.

> "My grace is sufficient for you, for my power is made perfect in weakness. Therefore I will boast all the more gladly about my weaknesses, so that Christ's power may rest on me." 2 Corinthians 12:9

Another time I actually saw a sign was several months later when we landed at the airport in Aruba for our summer vacation. Again, this may seem like a crazy coincidence, but to me it was a miraculous sign, even a funny one. I just know how it made me feel. It was that rush of spirit. We were walking through the little airport terminal when my eyes became focused on a man operating a cart with a pallet of hundreds of cans of "Cento" tomatoes. My mom was a fantastic cook, and she always said to me, "Ruth Anne, when you make sauce, you have to use Cento canned tomatoes. They are the best." She would kiss her fingers like a famous chef when describing something good. When I saw those cans of Cento tomatoes all piled up, I heard her voice and saw her kissing her fingers. I started exclaiming to Jeff, "Cento tomatoes! That's Ma!" He must have thought I was crazy.

"What the Heck are you talking about?" he said." I tried to explain it, but I'm not really sure how it came out. Yes, he probably did think I was crazy.

The last time I felt this overwhelming spirit of peace come over me was again when I was frantically seeking some presence of my mom. It was early one morning when I was doing a sewing project. I was sitting on the floor of my sewing room with pieces of fabric all over the place. I wanted, no, needed to talk to her about some questions I had about quilting. The need to talk to her became frantic and I hysterically started crying again. "Mom, I miss you. Where are you? I want to talk to you. Can you see me; can you hear me?" With that I looked up through my tears around my sewing room. Everywhere I looked I saw her....her fabrics, and her little boxes filled with pieces of cut out shapes she had made preparing for some sort of new quilting projects. Some were shapes of hearts, triangles or hexagons. I saw her sewing machine. I looked up and heard a voice saying, "Look all around. I am here, but I am inside of you." That hit me with such force and I grabbed my hands together and brought them to my heart. "That's right Mom. You are here. Somehow you are inside of me; who, I am. The things I can do are all because of the things you taught me and how you lived your life."

Please do not misunderstand. The voice I heard was not some distinct replica of my mother's voice. Again, I don't believe in communicating with the dead. It was just an inner thought, or perhaps the voice of the Holy Spirit. This profound inner thought was very real to me and it comforted me right on the spot!

December, 2016

I am now sixty three years old. I have come to the time where I feel that I need to wrap up this short book of memoirs of my journey with Parkinson's disease. I have some sense of urgency to do so. I don't know why. As the days progress, some are good and some are really bad. Maybe I just want to express myself before I am no longer able to. Maybe that will never happen. I pray it won't. Everything I have researched and read about Parkinson's and learned from my doctors says the progression won't stop with today's therapies. We may be able to slow it down with a good regime of drugs and other therapies, but the brain cells continue to degenerate, and can't be replaced.

The quality of my life is bound to be affected drastically as time goes by. All the things that in the beginning seemed so foreign when I was first diagnosed are now a part of my everyday reality. Without going into detail some of those changes are the dyskinesia is much worse, in fact ridiculously worse. The movement can be painful and exhausting. My "clicking off" episodes are much more dramatic and can last longer. During these times, the "FOG" (failure of gait) becomes a total failure and I am unable to walk. My whole demeanor changes and it's hard to hide it from people. I feel a whole change come over, like a black cloud or a mask. It takes a lot of concentration to talk and do things. Everything is in slow motion, and I just feel like sleeping. Then the meds click in and in a moment's notice, I am back. It's a heck of a way to live, but it's my life. I really have no choice, but to make the best of it and have faith that it's just part of a bigger plan that I will understand beyond what I know right now.

I am so grateful, because as of this writing, I am still working, enjoying my family, sewing, creating, and am fairly independent. When I need help, it's always there. My family is there for me, and comes running if I'm in trouble, which because of my stubbornness and fight, hasn't happened very often.

As I think back to the possibility of being in a wheelchair in five years, after my first neurological exam, I feel so blessed. I am truly amazed at how well I am doing. Others may not think so as they observe my sometimes awkward spastic movements, or my inability to walk. But, all things considered, so far I am winning the battle. At least, I am ahead for now. I don't know what tomorrow will bring. Only God knows, and I have great confidence in Him to be my citadel.

> *"For I am convinced that neither death nor life; neither angels nor demons, neither the present nor the future, nor any powers, neither height nor depth, nor anything else in all creation, will be able to separate us from the love of God that is in Christ Jesus our Lord." Romans 8:38-39.*

My co-workers, supervisors, and students at the community college where I teach ESL part time are the best. They are always supportive and treat me with dignity and respect. They have gone the extra mile to accommodate some of my needs. I am very open about my "affliction", so there are not too many surprises for my students and co-workers. I have been at this job for twenty-one years.

I believe I am one of the lucky ones because recently at my last check up with my neurologist, my doctor said that I am not just **one** of the most stable patients they have, but **THE** most stable patient that they have ever had. I am defying the odds. I have had PD for over twenty-six years. I can't even remember life without it.

One of my physicians whom I have become very close with is the coordinator for DBS surgery (Deep Brain Stimulation). This surgery involves putting a small pace maker type device in the chest and having electrical leads or sensors going into the brain. The patient has to be awake during the surgery. I don't even want to go into detail. They think I would benefit from it, but I am not even close to going for that. I kiddingly asked my doctor if they would have to shave my head. She laughed at me for my vanity.

I know that DBS has been very successful for many people. It's just personal with me. I have to feel it in my gut. I still think I am doing quite well, and to be fair, my doctors think I'm doing well too. They have my best interests at heart.

I don't believe that I am doing well because of anything that I have done right, but because my journey was mapped out by someone greater than myself; a God who loves me. I know this in my heart. I feel His presence when I am scared and at my wit's-end. At this point, I have fallen many times, when I am too impatient and think I can make it and I don't make it to the point of finding a solid surface to catch me. It's never been serious. But He has been there protecting me and holding my hand. I have called out to Him from the depths of my soul; I feel his love surrounding me when my fear wants to envelop me and take over all that is good. When I am afraid to walk, I step back and remember these words from the Book of Psalms.

"Where does my help come from? My help comes from the Lord, the maker of Heaven and Earth. He will not let your foot slip. He who watches over you will not slumber." Psalm 121:1-3.

I don't know what the future holds. Am I still holding out for a miracle? I would be lying if I said I wasn't. What I do know is that I am ok today. I am open to what God has in store for me.

When I decided to write a book, I didn't really know what form it would take. I just started writing it a long time ago, and I'm still able to write and tell my story. This should be an encouragement to those who have recently been diagnosed with Parkinson's or aspects of Parkinson's which is what I believe that I have. There is life after a diagnosis of Parkinson's. Ask the students in my class, or my husband, children, and especially my grandchildren. I swim, I play in the mud, I go for walks, make play dough, lots of messes, and am still the best playmate! I cook, sew, dance at weddings, and believe it or not, I can still play the piano, which is where this story began. I don't play as well as I used to, but I can still make music!

What started as an informative personal account of my experience with Parkinson's really turned into a journey of faith. I believe that is what my life is all about, a journey of faith.

Well now it is 1:00 am and I think I better put this thing to bed. I have to go to sleep so that I have enough strength for battle, the battle of a life stricken with Parkinson's disease. I will fight the good fight, keep the faith, and pray to be a blessing in my relatively small world.

At the beginning of my story, I used nicer words, like managing the disease, or living with PD, but now I write, **"BATTLE!"** Those who have Parkinson's know what I mean. Those heroes who have advanced Parkinson's no matter what age they may be are fighting hard, for their bodies, minds, and souls. We need better drug therapies, more research.

I thank other heroes too. Those who are fighting the battle with science and research like the Michael J. Fox Foundation, and the Parkinson's Unity Walk in Central Park. My team, "Drowning PD," will be there again this April, and hopes to raise over $15,000.00. We have exceeded our goals in the past and as of this writing, have raised over $61,000.00 for this great cause. My involvement in this grass roots fundraiser has helped give purpose to my life with Parkinson's. Being pro-active in raising funds to help put an end to this disease somehow helps me cope.

As I went about editing my writing, I noticed that even though the disease has progressed, I seem to be in a better place today. I think that I have moved into acceptance. My progression has been unusually slow, which I am grateful for.

After my diagnosis over twenty-six years ago I mentioned the heartache I felt over the fear of not being able to attend my children's graduations, and dance at their weddings. I proudly attended the college graduations of my three children and have danced at two of their weddings. As of this writing, Megan is still single but I look forward to dancing at her future wedding, if God allows.

$\mathcal{F}$inal Thoughts

At this point, I would like to ask your forgiveness if you find errors in my writing, usage of words, punctuation, capitalization, typing, etc. I have edited my writing so many times. I think I have at least eleven revisions to my story. It really is quite a challenge to get it right when you do it by yourself. I am so stubborn that I really didn't want any outside help. I didn't want anyone to change my words.

To finish this chapter of my journey, I will say that I am no longer afraid of the future. I think I will continue to put my feelings in writing. Maybe in another ten years I will have a different perspective. Who knows, if God allows, maybe there will be a sequel. Stop laughing! Even if no one reads my story, it feels good to express myself in writing.

It is pretty certain that there will come a time when I will no longer be able to write. Nothing I can do will be able to fight the insidious creeping in of old age; especially old age with Parkinson's and acceptance will come with a price.

Hopefully, my descendants will think of me as a woman of faith, who loved God and her family with an unwavering spirit, never gave up hope, and oh yes...... She had Parkinson's disease.

$\mathcal{E}$pilogue

November 2016

I had just put the last period on the last sentence of my story when I excitedly ran down to the family room to tell Jeff that I was finished!

As I came to the bottom of the stairs I "clicked off". With no warning, I took a huge tumbling fall. Surprisingly enough, I wasn't hurt, just my emotions were wounded. It was such a shock to me because it happened so fast. Usually I have a little warning as the changes occur. Jeff chastised me by asking, "Why didn't you wait until you were clicked on?"

I tearfully responded, "I was clicked on!" One second I was, and the next I wasn't. It is so difficult to understand.

Just a few weeks later, I was carrying a laundry basket filled with clothes up the same flight of stairs. There are only five stairs going to the main floor of our split level home. But when you are at the top of the stairs and the prospect of falling down them is realized, it looks like a long fall. When I got to the top of the stairs, for some reason, my feet were not planted correctly and I knew I was going to take a huge fall. I lost my balance, and screamed. Jeff was sitting on the couch and saw the whole thing. As I was falling down the stairs, I felt like I was being hoisted high up in the air, like some force was lifting me. The bottom of the stairs looked really far away. It was almost like I was an observer watching this scene take place. It all happened in a split second. When I landed, I was sitting in the most poised and comfortable position. Jeff will attest to this. One leg was straight out and the other was bent so that my legs looked like a number 4 position, if you can figure that out. It is actually a yoga pose. I was sitting up very straight, which I don't usually do. It looked like I had been placed there. I was not hurt in the least bit. I believe in Guardian Angels.

Even though I believe my Guardian Angel saved me from really hurting myself, this was still a nasty reminder that my journey with Parkinson's is not over. Things are going to keep changing, as the progression continues. I will hold tight to my family and God, and that possibility of being cured. My Guardian Angel will be working over- time.

I thank my family for letting me tell our story. It is extremely painful to share the sometimes ugly truth of what Parkinson's has done to me and the people I love. Yet I remind myself that it hasn't been all bad. I mentioned before that as the disease racks my body, my heart and spirit are growing and I feel so much better in that sense. Maybe this is my healing.

It is only because of their love that I have been able to write about my journey living with Parkinson's. In fact, just the other day I was playing with Nick. He wanted me to go outside with him. As I got up, I told him I wasn't sure if I could walk yet, and he responded, "I will help you walk. I will hold your hand. I will **always** help you walk."

Who could ask for anything more?

"And now, these three remain: faith, hope, and love. But the greatest of these is love." I Corinthians 13

May 15, 2018

After I finished "My Happy Feet" and self-published it, I had this incredible urge to write a novel with the development of Parkinson's into the plot.

"Chasing the Sunrise" is a novel that spans five generations of a family that began with Sophia and Nicholas Lipinski; Polish Immigrants who came to America in 1925. The story centers on Veronica Simms, granddaughter of Sophia and Nicholas. Veronica is a world renowned concert pianist who after a diagnosis of Parkinson's disease fights to hold on to everything that is important to her. The other characters fight their own battles. Theirs is a story of faith, love, passion, loss, gain, forgiveness, sacrifice, and redemption.

I fell in love with the characters that I created and I hope the reader will as well.

Look for "Chasing the Sunrise." It is available at www.lulu.com. You can find it in "Fiction: Love and Relationships"

Thank you for reading my story.

Lightning Source UK Ltd.
Milton Keynes UK
UKHW040158030922
408251UK00002B/339

9 781483 486154